Drama Lessons: Ages 7–11

Drama Lessons: Ages 7–11 offers an exciting and varied range of tried and tested lessons tailor-made for busy teachers. *Drama Lessons: Ages 7–11* emerges from the continuing positive responses to *Drama Lessons for Five to Eleven Year Olds* (2001). In this book you will find a carefully chosen selection of the best lessons from the original book, plus some exciting new material – a combination of brand new and classic lessons. This new collection introduces *Literacy Alerts* which identify how the drama activities develop aspects of literacy and suggest additional literacy activities. For each lesson plan, essential resources and timing information are provided. The lessons cover a range of themes and curriculum areas.

Full of pick-up-and-go lesson plans, this book will be of enormous interest to specialists and non-specialists of drama alike. All primary teachers, literacy coordinators and teaching assistants should have this book in their hands and it will give all trainee teachers a flying start in their school placements.

Judith Ackroyd is Dean of the Faculty of Humanities, Arts and Social Sciences at Regent's College, London.

Jo Barter-Boulton is Senior Lecturer in the School of Education at the University of Northampton.

Drama Lessons: Ages 7–11

Second Edition

**Judith Ackroyd and
Jo Barter-Boulton**

Routledge
Taylor & Francis Group

LONDON AND NEW YORK

First published as *Drama Lessons for Five to Eleven year olds* 2001
By David Fulton Publishers

This second edition published 2013
by Routledge
2 Park Square, Milton Park, Abingdon, Oxon OX14 4RN

Simultaneously published in the USA and Canada
by Routledge
711 Third Avenue, New York, NY 10017

Routledge is an imprint of the Taylor & Francis Group, an informa business

British Library Cataloguing in Publication Data
A catalogue record for this book is available from the British Library

Library of Congress Cataloging in Publication Data
A catalog record for this book has been requested

ISBN: 978-0-415-67783-7 (pbk)
ISBN: 978-0-203-80805-4 (ebk)

Typeset in Helvetica by Fakenham Prepress Solutions, Fakenham, Norfolk NR21 8NN

MIX
Paper from
responsible sources
FSC® C004839

Printed and bound in Great Britain by the MPG Books Group

Contents

Acknowledgements

We wish to thank the teachers, students and colleagues who have excited us with their drama work for children. Thanks also to those who have helped shape our own practice over many years: Gavin Bolton, David Booth, Dorothy Heathcote, Carole Miller, Jonothan Neelands, Cecily O'Neil, John O'Toole, Juliana Saxton and Philip Taylor. Bruce Roberts and James Hobbs at Routledge have been a delight to work with – we are most grateful.

We would like to thank Northamptonshire teacher Maureen Micklethwaite and her mother for their story and for copies of original documents with permission to use them. They provide context for Chapter 9, World War II: The Home Front. The authenticity they provide really enhances the learning experience for children.

We would also like to acknowledge Nelson Thornes for permission to reproduce an extract from *The Terrible Fate of Humpty Dumpty* by David Calcutt and Cambridge University Library for Nina de Garis Davies' *Ancient Egyptian Paintings*.

Thank you to our artist Charlie.

Introduction

This book emerges from the warm reaction to *Drama Lessons for Five to Eleven Year Olds* published in 2001 and the three books in the *Role Play in the Early Years* series published in 2004. These were written in response to the interest of teachers and students who were keen to use drama in their teaching and wanted more user-friendly material. Rather than simply producing a second edition of *Drama Lessons for Five to Eleven Year Olds*, we wished to produce two distinctive age-specific texts to ensure teachers get more appropriate material for their book/buck! Hence, in addition to this book, *Drama Lessons: Ages 7–11*, there is a sister text, *Drama Lessons: Ages 4–7*.

Again, we have chosen to concentrate purely on drama lesson plans rather than theorizing drama practice. A selection of useful publications is listed at the back of this book. The two new books feature some old favourites from the published four books alongside some previously unpublished materials. We are writing primarily for those teachers who have had little or no experience of teaching drama, but who have an interest in the subject and a willingness to have a go at lessons devised, tried and tested by other teachers. Experienced teachers may appreciate some new materials to add to their repertoire.

The dramas in this book are designed to fulfil a range of learning objectives in various curriculum areas and develop particular literacy skills through a creative curriculum approach. All dramas feature *Literacy Alerts*, which are identified by these icons: and to highlight opportunities for literacy learning. We have focused on *Literacy Alerts* as we want to foreground the importance of drama as a way of developing and enriching literacy skills across the primary curriculum. This icon identifies the literacy skills being developed by the drama activity. This icon identifies suggestions for additional literacy work that can be developed from the dramas.

The book provides all the information necessary for teachers to pick up and teach, with the authorial voice speaking directly to you, the teacher. Dramatic approaches are explained as they are used in the chapters. In addition, a glossary with instructions for a few useful drama games are provided. The resources required are listed and estimated times for each lesson are given. These times cannot be exact because different children respond differently to the same stimuli and therefore an activity can take as much as thirty minutes more with one group than another.

Each drama is made up of a sequence of activities, most of which need to be followed in the order given. We are aware that teachers are working in different spaces with different children and with different constraints. The book is therefore designed so that teachers can do as much or as little of the drama at any one time as is appropriate. Sometimes teachers may choose to include fifteen minutes of drama activity in a group session while others may choose to teach a whole drama during a half-day session.

We are delighted to have been given the opportunity to share more drama adventures with you and your children.

Teachers' notes

The layout of the book

Each plan is introduced with the following:

- **A brief synopsis** – a few lines outlining the story.
- **Learning objectives** – key areas we want children to know or understand by the end of the lesson. These are cross curricular and are not exhaustive. Many specific literacy learning moments are identified elsewhere in the Literacy Alerts (see below).
- **Themes** – again, these are cross curricular.
- **Resources** – provides a list of what you will need to deliver the lesson.
- **Timing** – suggested timings for the drama if the lesson was taught in one session. All groups are different and some teachers may choose to do only one short activity at a time. This may depend on the age of the children, their experience of drama and the organization of the school day.

The lesson plans are then divided into sections. Each section includes the following:

- **Teacher's intentions** – these explain the thinking behind the drama activity selected.
- **Type of activity** – explains what the children will be doing.

- **Literacy Alerts** ✏ – these *Literacy Alerts* highlight very specific literacy learning that should take place during the drama activity, e.g. prediction. ✏➕ This symbol highlights additional literacy activities which may take place before, during or even after the drama. These are not essential for teaching the main drama.

- **Reflection activities** – at the end of each lesson we have included opportunities for the children to reflect on what they have learned through the drama. These reflection activities may be through further drama work or through questions and discussion.

Delivering the dramas

Teacher in role

The dramas included in this book engage the teacher working in role. This does *not* mean that you have to use exaggerated voices or funny walks. Costumes and props are not necessary, although we provide suggestions of what might be used to help the children to distinguish between you as the teacher and you in role. It is important that you make it very clear when you are in role to avoid confusion. A hat can be quickly put on and taken off when you move between teacher and role, for example. All the teacher roles can be male or female, so you can change the names if you like, or you can play a different gender.

Choosing the drama activities appropriate for your class

All these dramas could be used across the 7–11 age range. The more the children participate in drama activities, the more comfortable and confident they will become.

Some of the games described from page xvi are specifically used in these dramas because they develop relevant skills. However, these games can all be used independently. Many teachers like to play a game prior to starting their dramas.

Preparing to teach

It is essential to read the lesson plan all the way through before starting. This will enable you to prepare the space and any required resources. You may also wish to select any

of the additional literacy activities indicated by the icon .

The plans can be adapted if you feel that you would like to give more time to some activities or place more emphasis on some of the sections. You may choose to do just one activity for a few minutes.

Once you have used some of the dramatic activities through teaching the lessons provided, you may wish to select some from the Glossary to use in your own planning. You may also like to look at the other drama books recommended at the back of the book, which will give you more ideas.

Before starting you may wish to agree a signal with the children which you will use to gain their attention, such as a hand raised, or a countdown: *3, 2, 1, freeze!*

Glossary

The glossary of the dramatic terms used in this book is not necessary to teach the activities in these chapters, since each activity is fully explained in the text. However, the glossary provides explanations of a range of the dramatic approaches used in the book and may help those who, having used them in these dramas, wish to plan their own drama sessions. We hope therefore that our notes on what the different activities can achieve and why we might choose to use them might be helpful.

Collective drawing and map making

Individuals add detail to a picture or map. Children come forward one or two at a time and draw on to the basic outline, which has been prepared by the teacher. Sometimes it will be quicker to give each child a piece of paper or a post-it note on which to draw. These individual drawings can then be stuck on to the outline picture. Alternatively, groups might be given parts of a complete picture or map to work on. These are then brought together to create one large illustration that all children have contributed to. This way of working gives the finished product collective ownership. If time is restricted, the picture can be finished later.

Collective or collaborative storytelling

The whole class joins in with the telling of the story. The teacher leads the storytelling and invites individuals to supply words, sound effects, phrases or whole sentences. This way the detail is provided by the children while the development of the plot is controlled by the teacher.

Conscience alley or thought tunnel

This invites children to examine a moment in the drama in detail. It is employed most effectively when a decision has to be made, or when a decision has already been irrevocably made. Sometimes it requires the children to offer advice to a character, too. Children consider what they or the character might think about the decision and its implications.

The children stand in two lines facing each other about a metre apart. The teacher walks very slowly from one end of the 'alley' or tunnel to the other. As she does so, she turns to the child to one side and then to the other. They speak aloud a word or line (e.g. to Goldilocks, *You should leave this cottage*).

The thought tunnel offers a way of speaking a character's thoughts, rather than offering advice. The character moves through the tunnel in exactly the same way (e.g. as Goldilocks, *I should leave this cottage*).

Alleys or tunnels can be curved to represent the context, such as a winding path, and straight to represent the corridor leading to an important room. However, straight lines enable children to see and hear each other better.

Costuming

Selected props or items of clothing are chosen by the teacher to indicate a particular role to a class. It is important that any costume is put on in front of the children so they observe the teacher going into role in front of them. This ensures that there is no confusion about who the teacher actually is. Sometimes, with younger children, you can let them help you to put on items of clothing, helping with fastenings and giving advice as to which way around they go or which item to put in first. In many dramas the items are not immediately visible, so that the children bring them out of a bag or box one by one, guessing who might own such items.

Defining space

This is the way in which the teacher and class agree on the parameters and features of the fictional space. In the process the classroom space is defined as the place in the drama. It might be agreed that when we are facing the window side of the classroom we are facing the sea and the other side is inland. Items of furniture might be used to define the space. Two chairs, for example, might be used to define the gateposts leading to the castle. Children enjoy being part of the decision-making process and this enhances their commitment.

Discussion in role

Here the teacher and the children are in role discussing an issue or problem inside the drama. The conversation is not *about* the characters (e.g. *What do you think frightens him?*) but *between* the characters (e.g. *Do you understand why I am frightened?*). The discussion takes place *as if* the teacher and children are other people in another place; in a fictional context. Discussion in role may be set up as a formal meeting held to sort out problems or discuss plans. See **Meetings**.

Dramatic construction

We have used this term to describe moments when the children physically 'become' something inanimate – a bridge, a forest or a castle wall. It may be used to set the scene for action or to introduce an objective view on action. The forest trees, for example, can warn a deer that she is being followed or encourage her to run faster.

Dramatic play

Here children are indulging in imaginative play, but in the context of the shared drama. They may be preparing some food, making a toy or painting a rocket. The action is not controlled by the teacher, but the teacher may wander around among the children asking them about what they are doing as though she, too, is involved in the fiction: *What flavour is your cake going to be? How will you make that? How did you reach to paint that top bit?*

The children have freedom for individual creativity and are involved in their own worlds, so that one is baking a cake in a kitchen while another is shopping for drinks. High levels of concentration or emotion are not necessary in dramatic play, though of course they may occur. The activity helps to build up belief in the fiction. It is particularly useful with younger children.

Freeze frames/frozen pictures/still images/tableaux

We do not distinguish between these terms in this book. To make *freeze frames*, children arrange themselves as though they are in a three-dimensional picture, depicting a scene or a particular moment. It creates a frozen moment when we imagine time has stopped, giving us the opportunity to look at it more closely.

Freeze frames may be created by small groups, or by the whole group when they are often referred to as Collective still images or Collective Frozen pictures. They may be created quickly in the count to five, or they may be built one person at a time. This slower image-building approach enables children to respond to what others are doing in the image by placing themselves in a position that relates to another's. A child seeing someone else in an image on a swing in a park may stand behind the swing as though he is pushing it higher. Figures in freeze frames can be tapped on the shoulder and asked questions or their thoughts about something or someone in the drama. Freeze frames can be brought to life so they move into dramatic play and then frozen again with a clap of the hands. They can be reformed to show the future or the past. Captions can be voiced or written for freeze frames giving titles or moods. They are very flexible and are used often in these dramas in different ways.

Hot seating

Here one person in role as a character is asked questions by the rest of the class. The teacher is usually the best person to have in a hot seat since the pressure can be high. Also, the hot seat is often used to provide information, so the teacher is the one who can do this. An example might be the teacher on the hot seat being asked about how a canal is built. The children do not have the information and the teacher wants them to ask questions in order to learn. Hence, it is helpful as a way to give information to children without being 'the teacher'. The children can ask questions directly to a character in a hot seat to find out whatever they wish to know. This requires them to think of the most appropriate questions and sometimes the best way of asking them. Sometimes there may be fictional pressure on them in the drama to find out all they can – if you don't know how canals are built, you will not get a job and there will be no money to support the family. This heightens their motive to find out and the teacher's history lesson is achieved! Children may ask as themselves or in role as others in the drama.

Improvisation

The children act and speak in role. There is no pre-planning. Improvisation is often led by the teacher in role enabling her to keep control of the direction of the improvisation. All involved are speaking as characters in the drama.

Interviewing

Quite simply, the children and perhaps teacher are engaged in interviewing each other in role. Sometimes this can be carried out with children in pairs of A and B. They can take it in turns of being the interviewer. The roles of interviewers may be helpers who wish to understand someone or a situation better, or could be press or television journalists. Those being interviewed will be characters from the drama.

Meetings

This highly structured activity engages the teacher and children together in role, gathered for a specific purpose. This may be to hear new information, make plans or discuss strategies. The teacher will usually be the chair or leader at the meeting so that he can order the proceedings and ensure all the children's views are heard. Formal meetings are enhanced by an arrangement of chairs or benches in appropriate rows, and perhaps an agreed action when the Chair enters the room. Decisions about pace and procedures will depend upon the context of the meeting.

Narration and narration with mimed action

Teacher narration in drama activities is a useful strategy for setting the scene or moving the action along. It is often a very useful controlling device! The teacher is empowered to dictate particular aspects of the drama. A class working noisily, for example, may hear the teacher narrate, '*Gradually, they fell silent. The helpers were too tired to speak.*' Narration is also used to excite interest and build tension in the drama (e.g. *No one knew what was inside the bag. Some wondered if it might contain secrets while others felt sure it contained the lost treasure*). It may be used to set the scene (e.g. *The hall was enormous and richly decorated*) or to move the action forward (e.g. *They all packed their bags and started out on the dangerous journey*).

We enjoy drawing the children into narration through mimed action. *The villagers had to climb up over high rocks on their journey*, for example, would be accompanied by everyone miming climbing over imaginary rocks. It may also be used to help the children to imagine they are all one character (e.g. *She put on her big strong boots, tying the laces tightly. She then put on a heavy coat and did up the buttons, one, two, three and four*). Each child, in his or her own space, will mime the actions as the teacher narrates.

The opportunities for engaging children in the narration are described under **Storytelling** below.

Overheard conversations

Children in groups make up conversations that people in their drama may have had. They then overhear one another's conversations as though they are eavesdropping. This enables the children to work in small groups and gives all of them the chance to comment in role on the action of the drama. The easiest way to set this up is for the groups to have time improvising first, before being asked to fall silent. You then wander around the room stopping to eavesdrop on the groups in turn. In this way, all the children are actually eavesdropping since they are all quiet. They are also waiting for the moment when you stand near them and they must have their conversation. As you walk away from them they fade out and the group you approach start their conversation. It is fun if you move away in mid-sentence to create some suspense. When you return to the group they will pick up where they left off and more is revealed to the class.

Ritual

Ritual is a repeated procedure that those in the drama are familiar with and value highly. In drama a ritual is used to give action significance. Any action, no matter how mundane, may be performed in a formal and dignified manner to make the actions seem to matter. Putting items into a picnic basket, for example, by having one child at a time step forward to place an imaginary contribution into the basket announcing what it is, brings about a more serious level of thought to the action and a more exciting atmosphere. While not a ritual in the strictest sense, it creates attention and status to the action.

Role on the wall

The outline of a character in the drama is drawn on to a large sheet of paper. This could even be a stick figure if you are not very confident drawing. Information about the character in the drama is collected and written around the outline. It is possible to contrast different types of information in a role on the wall. What the character says can be written in one colour and what she thinks in another. Sometimes the character's thoughts are written in the round head of the role on the wall and what other people think about the character is written around the outside of the figure.

Sculpting

This way of working involves children making statues of each other or the teacher through suggestions and/or physical manipulation. Sculptures can be made to crystallize ideas about a character, such as what the bully looked like; or to express a feeling, such as how anger could be physically represented. Children might suggest that the bully holds her head higher or has a hand on the waist. Sculpting enables different ideas to be seen represented. The class may wish to agree one particular stance at the end of their exploration.

Sound collage/soundscapes

Soundscapes are created by the children. This can be achieved in different ways. A sound collage may accompany a journey with sounds accompanying the group or teacher in role climbing a mountain or travelling through a forest at night. Children might represent the features of the forest, as a tree with rustling branches or an owl hooting. Sound collages are creative and provide an opportunity for those not so confident in speaking out loud to participate orally. The sounds can also be made using objects or musical instruments.

Statementing

Statementing involves the children in making statements about a person, event or place in the drama. The statements may be made in a ritualistic manner, with children stepping forward one at a time to give their statement. They may remain frozen in a gesture appropriate to the statement while others make their statements, or they may return to their original place and watch the others. It is a way of involving the children in the construction or consideration of events or characters so that they have a sense of ownership. It can be useful to slow the drama down with some serious thought, such as statements about what people would say about the girl who has just stolen a pencil case.

Still images/freeze frames/frozen pictures/tableaux

We do not distinguish between these terms in this book. See *Freeze frames* for detailed description.

Storytelling

This activity includes different modes of storytelling. Sometimes the teacher provides narration with pauses that the children fill in, as described above under *Collaborative storytelling*. This involves them in the storytelling and makes their contribution part of the whole. At other times storytelling is suggested as a way to involve all the children in reviewing the events of the drama. Here each child takes it in turns to tell a line of the story, as in a story circle. Older children may divide into small groups to story tell the events of their drama together.

Teacher in role

The teacher takes the role of someone in the drama. This enables the teacher to work with the children from inside the drama. Additional information may be given through the teacher's role, as described in *Hot seating* above, for example. A teacher in role can pose questions to challenge the children's ideas and assumptions. Discipline can be maintained through the teacher in role, which is usually more effective and less disruptive than when we discipline as teachers. For example, if children are being noisy, teacher in role explains that since the recent events she has suffered from terrible headaches and she won't be able to tell them where the treasure lies unless they speak quietly. Or, for example, the pharaoh mustn't wake up, so we will all have to whisper. Teacher in role is used in many approaches listed in this glossary, such as meetings, hot seating, whole-class improvisation and dramatic play.

Thought tracking and thought tapping

Thought tracking enables children in role to speak aloud the thoughts that would normally remain concealed. This can be done in different ways, such as **Conscience alleys** or **thought tunnels**, described above. The thoughts of characters could also be tracked during a mime. Another form of thought tracking might be created by placing an object or character in the centre of a circle of children who offer advice or thoughts.

Thought tapping is when the teacher literally taps a child on the shoulder as a signal for the child to speak the thoughts of the character he is playing. Thought tapping is also used in conjunction with mimed activity or most commonly with freeze frames. Once the children are doing either of these, the teacher moves among them and taps them on the shoulder one at a time. She may ask about what the children are doing, about what they are thinking or feeling, or about what they can see or smell or hear from where they are. It invites children to commit further to their roles and to the drama, and to think further about the context. Their contributions become part of the shared understanding of the imaginary place and people. It is a quite controlled activity that gives less vocal individuals their moment.

Whole-group improvisation

This activity involves the children and the teacher working together in role. The teacher will have teacher intentions in mind, but the ideas and suggestions offered by the children, and therefore the responses of the teacher will vary when working with different groups. It is this mode of activity which often generates a high level of concentration and emotional commitment. Unlike dramatic play, the children are all engaged in one world, dealing with the same problem.

Drama games

A cleared space is needed for all these games and a circle of chairs is required for 'Fruit salad'.

Captain's coming!

The teacher explains the commands that the children must respond to. They imagine they are on board a large ship/sailing vessel. 'Captain's coming!' means that they all stand still with a straight back and a salute. 'Bombs overhead!' means that they lie on the floor face down with arms and legs straight. 'Scrub the decks!' means that they mime scrubbing the decks.

You can designate directions and include '*Port!*' and '*Starboard*'. You can use a few commands to begin with and build in more as the children get better at remembering and responding quickly.

The teacher or a child calls out the commands and the children get into the appropriate positions as quickly as possible. The last one into the correct position is out. The winner is the person left in at the end. Between commands, the children can move around the space not touching each other. You could play music such as a sea shanty and turn it down as you call the commands. If the children can dance the hornpipe they may do so between commands!

This is a fun, energetic activity. Children have to be ready to respond very quickly to instructions so it does require concentration. It encourages speedy reactions. You can adapt the game for different contexts. '*Teacher's coming!*' in a school-based drama might generate commands such as '*Line up*' and '*Sit in a circle*'. The children can make up commands for the game.

Fruit salad

The children sit on chairs in a circle. There should be no empty chairs. Each child is allocated one of three names (e.g. apple, mango or banana). A caller stands in the middle of the circle and calls out one of the fruits (e.g. mango), and all the mangoes have to leave their seats and rush to find another chair to sit on. The caller's aim is to sit on a chair too. Whoever is left without a chair is the next caller. If 'Fruit salad' is called, everyone has to leave their chairs and find another. Players are not allowed to return to the chairs they have just vacated. When their fruit is called they must find new chairs. The aim for everybody is to ensure they are sitting on a chair.

This game can be adapted to introduce different vocabulary relevant to the context of the drama, such as pyramid, pharaoh, Nile and sarcophagus in the drama 'Building the Pyramid'. Any names, terms or even descriptive words may be used. This is a fun way to introduce new or difficult vocabulary to children. New words introduced in the game will soon become familiar.

Grandmother's footsteps

Person A faces a wall at one end of the room and the children all face her at the other end. A turns around at random intervals. The children's aim is to creep up behind A without being seen to move when A looks around. The first to reach A taps her shoulder and wins the game. A's aim is to make sure that no one achieves this. The winner can take A's place.

This game is about physical control, concentration and challenge. It creates a building up of tension as people get nearer to A. A similar game is 'What's the time, Mr Wolf?'

This game could be used in 'Is Emma's Friend Stealing?' in preparation for the moment of theft.

Keeper of the keys

Person A sits blindfolded on a chair in the middle of the space. There is a bunch of keys or other jingling object beneath the chair. The others stand at some distance in a wide circle around the chair. Their aim is to get the keys. A's aim is to ensure that the keys remain under the chair.

Those around the edge must move as quietly as they can towards the chair. If A hears any sound, she points in the direction of the sound. Whoever is pointed at must move back to the perimeter of the circle and begin again. Whoever is able to grab the keys without being pointed at is the winner and takes the place of person A.

This can also be played with individuals approaching the chair one at a time.

This game involves physical control and coordination as well as concentration. It may be used with a different item under the chair that is relevant to the drama.

Chapter 1
The Lonely Dragon

There is a cave halfway up the mountain where a dragon lives. The villagers who live at the bottom of the mountain are not happy about the dragon and hide whenever they see him coming. One day they see him crying and decide to find out why he is so sad. The villagers find out about the dragon and befriend him.

Learning objectives

- To explore differences between people;
- To discuss the danger of jumping to conclusions about people;
- To work together to solve problems;
- To use dramatic techniques to explore characters and issues.

Themes

- Fear of the unknown
- Friendship
- Loneliness
- Being misunderstood.

Resources

- *Optional:* A large piece of 'dragon-coloured' material. Large sheets of paper and pens.

Time

- One hour.

Notes

The idea for this drama came originally from a book called *The Dragon Who Couldn't Help Breathing Fire* by Denis Bond. In this story the dragon's problem is that he breathes fire when he laughs and causes havoc wherever he goes. He eventually finds that he can be useful to people by lighting fires for them. This drama takes on the spirit of the story.

Figure 1.1 The dragon, by Charlie

The villagers live in fear

Teacher's intentions

- To build belief in the setting;
- To introduce the dragon as a threat to the village;
- To tell the beginning of the story collectively, using the children's ideas.

Brainstorm —what do we know about dragons? Think of words to describe dragons. Think of reasons why people might be afraid of dragons. Write these ideas on a large sheet of dragon-shaped paper

Discussion and narration: setting the scene

Tell the children that you are going to tell a story about a village that is situated at the bottom of a mountain. Ask the children to imagine what things they would see if they walked through the village. Would there be a park, a river, shops? Try to build up a clear picture of the village using words. Tell the beginning of the story:

Halfway up the mountain was a cave and in the cave lived a dragon. No one in the village liked the dragon. No one ever went up the mountain to see him. In fact, he never ever had any visitors.

Ask the children why no one ever visited the dragon. They may say things like:

- *He would eat them.*
- *He is frightening.*
- *He has big claws and might scratch them.*
- *He breathes fire.*

Whatever they suggest, try to emphasize that no one has ever seen the dragon do any of the bad things they are worried about. Lead a storytelling session, encouraging the children to fill in the details.

- *The people in the village were afraid of the dragon because they thought he might... (Eat them?)*
- *They believed he would ... (Stamp on their houses?)*
- *They were afraid he was going to... (Breathe fire?)*

Finish with:

- *They never saw him do any of these things, but they were always afraid he would.*

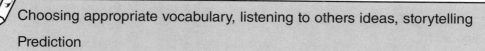

Choosing appropriate vocabulary, listening to others ideas, storytelling

Prediction

Read stories and poems about dragons

Collective drawing: the dragon

The whole class sits in a circle around a large sheet of paper and come forward, usually one at a time, to contribute to part of a drawing of a dragon. Individuals choose which part of the dragon they would like to draw and the colours to use. Keep the dialogue and questioning going while the children are coming one or two at a time to draw their part of the dragon. The finished dragon will be an exciting mix of the children's collective ideas. This could be done in groups or individually rather than with the whole class and discuss similarities and differences.

 Descriptive language, make suggestions

Individuals draw and label their own dragons. Children encouraged to use metaphor or simile to describe the dragon

Collect pictures of different dragons and stories about dragons to make a display

How do we feel when we see the dragon?

Teacher's intentions

- To continue to build belief in the village, and the threat felt by the villagers;
- To bring the village to life;
- To explore the feelings of the villagers.

Freeze frames: when the dragon comes

Tell the children that the dragon never comes very close to the people but he will sometimes be seen flying overhead and watching them. Ask the children to work in groups to produce a freeze frame of something that is happening in the village one sunny day. Ask children to suggest a few ideas first to make sure everyone has an idea of what they might be doing (e.g. playing football, going shopping, having a picnic by the river). Practise the freeze frame, remembering that people in freeze frames can't move or talk! Look at the freeze frames one at a time. Ask children to guess what is going on in each 'picture'. You are able to talk to the people in the freeze frame by touching them on the shoulder. Perhaps ask basic questions at first such as:

- *What are you doing?*
- *Who are you with?*
- *What are you holding in your hand?*
- *What's the weather like today?*

Ask the children to go back to their original freeze frame and then imagine how the picture would change if the dragon was to be seen flying towards them. Ask them to practise changing the freeze frame from one to the other. Look at each group in turn showing these two linked images. Again, it is possible to talk to the people in the picture by touching them on the shoulder. Ask questions such as:

- *What can you see?*
- *Tell me what it looks like.*
- *What can you hear?*
- *How do you feel?*
- *Why are you looking so frightened? What are you going to do now?*
- *What do you think the dragon might do?*

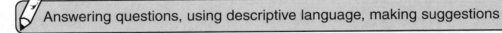

Answering questions, using descriptive language, making suggestions

Make a map of the village and annotate it

Draw pictures of themselves in role as the villagers. Write speech bubbles and thought bubbles for their roles

The village gathers for a celebration

Teacher's intentions

- To introduce sympathy for the dragon;
- To allow for group decision-making;
- To provide an opportunity for interaction between characters.

Whole-group improvisation: the great event is planned

Tell the children that there is going to be a big event happening on the village green that afternoon or evening. It could be linked in with a particular time of year if appropriate, such as bonfire night, summer fair, Diwali or May Day. Ask the children to suggest what could be happening and come to a collective decision. Ask the children to think of what would need to be prepared and organized for the event (e.g. food, decorations, entertainment). Tell the children that they are going to be working in the space, which is the village green/a field by the river. Children can work individually, in pairs or in small groups to get everything ready. The teacher can join in, in role as a villager, helping out where necessary with ideas and advice. Allow this to go on for as long as the children are engaged — this may be five or fifteen minutes! Give the agreed signal: *3, 2, 1, freeze!* When the children are 'frozen', continue the story:

As everyone was busy suddenly in the distance they saw the dragon flying slowly towards them. As they stood looking at the dragon they were utterly amazed to see tears rolling down his cheeks. He turned round and flew silently back to his cave.

Discussing and negotiation in a group to make a joint decision

Design a poster advertising the village event

Write a list: Decide on all the things that need to be done to prepare for the event. Write a list and choose which activity children will be involved in.

Discussion in role: what could be wrong with the dragon?

Ask the children to sit down. Still in role, begin to talk about what they have just seen.

Some may feel immediate sympathy for the poor dragon, others may be suspicious. Encourage discussion.

- *Did you see the dragon just now?*
- *Why do you think he was crying?*
- *He might just be tricking us.*
- *What do you think we should do?*
- *I feel bad about him, he looked so lonely.*

The children need to decide what they want to do about the situation. The drama could take a different direction from here depending on the children's decisions. The teacher could narrate if necessary:

After much discussion about what could be done, some of the villagers suggested that people should be sent to visit the dragon in his cave to find out what was the matter.

It is better from an organizational and classroom management point of view if all of the villagers go. However, if only some of the children volunteer, you may decide to allow the others to watch the proceedings. Those who choose to go can then report back once they have visited the dragon. The children may decide to send the dragon a letter or an invitation, but there is the problem that perhaps he can't read so someone will have to take it to him just in case. Decide what needs to be said to the dragon and what questions they want answered.

 Discussion, different viewpoints, framing questions

Write an invitation to the dragon

Write a list of synonyms for the word sad. These can be collected on a picture of a sad dragon's face

The journey to the dragon's cave

Teacher's intentions

- To represent the journey using movement and description;
- To add anticipation and tension to the story.

Dramatic construction and sound collage: the path up the mountain

Explain to the children that they are going to represent the path up the mountain to the dragon's cave. Ask them to stand in two lines, facing each other. They can bend the lines slightly to indicate the twists and turns in a real mountain path. Ask them to think of a physical object that they might see along that path (e.g. a tree, a bush, a rock, a stream). Ask the children to stand in a way that represents that object (e.g. crouched down for a rock, arms outstretched for a tree). Children could decide on a sound effect their object could make. Walk along the path, pausing in front of each object and hear the children make their sounds creating a sound collage. You can also give precise instructions as to how the sounds are to be made (e.g. everyone whisper their sounds). This journey can be repeated a number of times in different ways to create different sound collages.

 Make appropriate contributions

Children think of a word or words to describe the object they are representing. You could make this instruction more specific (e.g. think of three adjectives or verbs to describe what you are without using the noun itself: *tall, leafy, swaying*). These could be written on a picture of the mountain or as a class poem

Meeting the dragon

Teacher's intentions

- To introduce the teacher in role;
- To ask and answer questions in role;
- To begin to explore misunderstandings and assumptions made about others.

Narration and teacher in role: the journey ends at the dragon's cave

Set up a chair which will be inside the dragon's cave. It adds atmosphere if the chair is covered in an appropriately coloured drape. Ask the children to sit outside the cave as if they have just arrived after their journey. Narrate:

After a difficult climb up the mountain past rocks and streams, trees and bushes, the villagers arrived at the dragon's cave. As they sat and waited they could hear a noise coming from inside the cave.

Tell the children you are going to be in role as the dragon. Sit on the chair and show through your body language and facial expression that you are not happy! Perhaps sniff loudly or blow your nose.

Hello? Is there anyone there? I can hear someone outside the cave. Don't hurt me.

Draw the children into conversation. The dragon is very lonely and has no friends. People are afraid of dragons because of stories which aren't always true. He has never eaten anyone and is a vegetarian who prefers the carrots he grows in his garden. No one ever speaks to him in the village and they always look frightened. He can't help looking scary. It's the way he was born. He only breathes fire when he laughs.

Hopefully, the children will tell the dragon their fears and realize they have no foundation. They often invite the dragon to come down to the village to join in the celebrations. The dragon takes advice about what to wear, and the children can discuss health and safety issues with him about the possibility of his breathing fire.

 Posing questions, responding to answers appropriately

The celebration!

Teacher's intention

- To see the situation from another's viewpoint.

Dramatic construction and thought tunnel, improvisation: the dragon goes to the celebration

Ask the children to re-create the path down the mountain. However, this time ask them to imagine how the dragon might be feeling as he walks slowly towards the village green. What are the thoughts going round in his head? As you walk past each one, this time in role as the dragon, pause so he or she can speak aloud what he or she imagines the dragon might be thinking:

- *I'm really excited.*
- *I hope they'll be nice to me.*

- *Perhaps it's a trick and they're going to kill me.*
- *I hope I don't knock anyone over with my tail.*

As you arrive at the end of the thought tunnel, turn around slowly and address the children as if they were the villagers.

Hello everyone. Thank you for inviting me. Is there anything I can do to help?

It may be suggested that the dragon helps to put up the balloons or even to light the bonfire or barbecue. The dragon will have to explain that he can't breathe fire unless someone makes him laugh. The villagers think of ways, such as pulling funny faces, telling jokes and tickling him with a feather. The dragon can decide what makes him laugh. The ending of the drama can be improvised or narrated:

The celebration went with a swing. Everyone enjoyed it, especially the dragon. From that day to this the people in the village have not been afraid of the dragon because they now know him and know that although he looks strange and different he is really a friendly dragon after all.

Use talk to convey complex emotions

Using talk to create and respond to situations

Write a list or annotate drawings of ways to make the dragon laugh

Collect dragon jokes, e.g.
Knock Knock
Who's there!
Dragon!
Dragon who?
Dragon your feet again!
Or jokes to make a dragon laugh

Write a newspaper article about the lonely dragon coming to the celebration

Write a diary entry for the dragon recalling his day out

Reflection: what have we learned?

- Why was the dragon lonely?
- How did the villagers feel about him at the beginning of the story?
- What happened to change their minds?
- Do we ever feel like the dragon did?

It is important that the wider implications of the story are discussed.

- What assumptions did the villagers hold?
- When do we make assumptions that are not accurate?

Recall information, give reasons for opinions, and discuss emotions

Collect happy and sad words. Think about words are describe the dragon at different points in the story. How did he feel when he flew towards the villagers? How did he feel at the end?

Speech and thought bubbles. What is the dragon thinking and feeling at different points in the story? Draw speech and thought bubbles. What he says and what he thinks may, of course, be different

Chapter 2
Red Riding Hood

This drama begins with the familiar story. Mother sends Red Riding Hood on an important errand. Granny, who lives on the other side of the wood, is poorly and Red Riding Hood takes a basket of goodies to cheer her up. However, when Red Riding Hood arrives at her Granny's house, she realizes that a wolf occupies her Granny's bed. A passing woodcutter rescues Red Riding Hood and her grandmother, and the wolf receives a punishment.

This incident causes distress and anxiety to the local villagers and forest dwellers. Does the wolf deserve to be punished? Is he sorry for what he has done? How will his family cope without him? Will security arrangements be changed in the forest after this incident?

Learning objectives

- To recognize right and wrong and what is fair and unfair;
- To recognize how behaviour affects other people;
- To share opinions and explain views.

Themes

- Keeping safe;
- Problem solving;
- Helping and caring for others;
- Moral and social dilemmas.

Resources

- A basket for Granny's goodies to be put into/or a large piece of paper with Granny's basket drawn on it (see Figure 2.1);
- Felt pens;
- Small pieces of paper and glue or post-its;
- Optional props for Granny and wolf (a shawl and a hat, for example).

Time

- One hour.

Notes

This drama uses the well-known traditional tale and explores certain issues from it. As class teacher you have to decide whether you want Granny and Red Riding Hood to be eaten by the wolf, or is Granny hiding in the wardrobe and is Red Riding Hood rescued just in time? We usually have them both eaten alive and unharmed, not chewed by the wolf, so that the woodcutter can turn the wolf upside-down and shake him – they fall out. Also, in our version, the woodcutter does not kill the wolf, so we are able to meet him later on and talk to him. An added twist is that the wolf is a family man and we can meet members of his family in the drama.

Telling our version of the story

Teacher's intentions

- To share the telling of the story;
- To offer individual ideas.

Collective storytelling: telling our version of the Little Red Riding Hood

If you can, find an appropriate written text then that can be used, but an oral retelling is preferable, as the children can help to tell the story. This will give them more collective ownership of the tale. What follows is based on the authors' version of the story.

Introduce the work by leading a storytelling session to make sure everyone is using the same version of the story as the basis of the drama. As there are clearly hundreds of alternative versions of the traditional story, emphasize that this is our special version and it may not be the same as other versions that the children have heard. Start with the traditional opening and set the scene.

Once upon a time, there lived a little girl whose name was Elizabeth. Everyone who knew Elizabeth called her Little Red Riding Hood because she always wore a red cloak with a hood that her granny had made for her. She lived with her mother and father in a little cottage in the middle of a wood.

After modelling the storytelling technique for a short while, give children opportunities to supply words or phrases to finish your sentences. Tell the children that you will look directly at the person who you want to give the next part of the story. This form of collective storytelling involves all of the children and ensures that they listen to the story because no one knows who will be asked to give the next idea.

At the specific moment in the story, when Red Riding Hood is packing the basket of goodies, use a real basket or the prepared picture of Granny's basket for the next activity.

Collective drawing and ritual: what goodies shall we take to Granny?

Children discuss what might be put in the basket. This can done simply with the children standing in a circle around either a real or an imaginary basket and coming forward one at a time to put their (imaginary) present in. Alternatively, each child draws a picture of a present to put in it. If you are using a picture of a basket, children can either draw objects on to the prepared picture, or they can draw objects on to post-it notes to be stuck on to the prepared picture (see Figure 2.1).

Figure 2.1 A basket to fill with goodies for Granny

Children stand around the basket in a circle and come forward one at a time to place items in the basket, while announcing what it is they are putting in and giving reasons:

- *I am putting a magazine in the basket for Granny for her to read ...*
- *A hot water bottle to keep her warm ...*
- *Medicine to make her better ...*
- *I am giving Granny some flowers. They smell nice.*
- *I think Granny would like a film to cheer her up.*

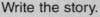 Storytelling: choosing appropriate words and phrases

Draw and label individual baskets for Granny.
Write the story.
Storyboard the story.
Make a list of characters in the story.

Collective storytelling: finish the story

Continue the collective storytelling, which could include the following points. It is crucial that the wolf is left alive.

- Red Riding Hood is warned by her mother not to talk to strangers;
- She stops to talk to some of her friends in the forest and the wolf overhears their conversation. These could be the woodland creatures such as Bill the Badger or Ollie the Owl, who delivers the post;
- The door to Granny's cottage is ajar when she arrives and the cottage is in darkness;
- The wolf swallows Red Riding Hood in one piece without chewing her at all;
- The woodcutter shakes the wolf and Red Riding Hood falls out unharmed, followed closely by Granny;
- Wolf is taken to prison or to the zoo, depending on how you feel about his behaviour.

Storytelling: using language to structure a story

 Draw a map from Red Riding Hood's house to Granny's. Write out directions

Make a collection of different book versions of the story. Collect other wolf stories

Shall I tell you what happened to me yesterday?

Teacher's intentions

● To hear a different perspective.

Storytelling in role and discussion: Granny tells her story

Tell the children that you are going to tell the story again as if you were one of the characters. Use some simple props or costume to indicate that you are in role as Granny. Sit on a chair, which is perhaps draped with material and can be known as the 'storyteller's chair' to make it sound a little more exciting. In role as Granny, briefly recall the events that happened in your cottage yesterday. It is quite fun if Granny is not a 'stereotypical' grandmother and is actually rather cheeky. She was not frightened by her ordeal and is thankful that the wolf didn't chew her up. What she didn't like was the smell of curry/garlic/salt and vinegar crisps in his stomach and also that his teeth were not brushed and were rotting.

Discuss what the children have learned from listening to Granny's story. What do we know now that we didn't know before?

Hot seating: asking Granny questions

Children are asked to decide on some questions to ask Granny to clarify what they have heard or collect further information.

 Listening to different viewpoints

 Collect information about Granny in a role on the wall. Write information we know in one colour and questions to ask Granny in another

Design a get well card for Granny

Storytelling: groups retell the story from different viewpoints

In groups of four, children tell the story round the group in role as one of the other main characters – the wolf, Red Riding Hood, the woodcutter. Discuss how these stories are different.

 Storytelling: using language to structure a story

Who will you be in the story?

Teacher's intentions

- Developing roles for the children;
- Building belief in the characters.

Creating roles: who's who?

Tell the children that they are all going to be characters in the story and they can choose who they would like to be. Unfortunately, the children cannot choose to be one of the main characters – Red Riding Hood, the wolf, the woodcutter, Granny – but they can decide to be someone who knows Granny or one of the other characters. They might be one of the people who live in the wood, perhaps a friend of Granny's, or one of the woodland animal friends of Red Riding Hood (such as a rabbit, owl, fox). If so, the children would be reminded to behave in a humanized manner, not growling and crawling on the floor! (It is great fun to include these characters though, as they add another dimension to the story. Particularly useful characters are Mrs Wolf and the wolf children.)

Ask the children to talk in pairs to decide who they are going to be in the drama and then to tell the whole group. They need to make it clear how they know the other characters from the wood and you may have to help them through some direct questioning.

- *I'm Mrs Wolf. I'm married to the wolf that ate Granny. He's not a bad chap really. I don't know why he did it.*
- *I'm Doris Starling. I know Granny from Bingo. She's a lovely lady.*
- *I live in the village and run the shop. I know everyone who lives here.*

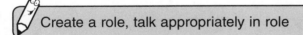

Create a role, talk appropriately in role

Create a character profile for your role

Hot seating: the teacher in role

Tell the children that it is a couple of days after the incident and Red Riding Hood is feeling very unsettled about what happened. She is afraid that some other awful things may happen. Ask the children if they will talk to her about what happened and try to reassure her. First they may ask some questions about the incident and then go on to reassure her about things to boost her confidence. What would they like to ask? Frame some questions in pairs or as a whole group. Perhaps write them down on the board to refer to. What can they say to reassure Red Riding Hood? How should they approach her? What tone of voice should they use?

Children in role as neighbours talk to teacher in role as Red Riding Hood and find out more information about her adventure with the wolf. They then go on to coax her into a walk in the woods or a visit to see some friends or something else to give her confidence.

Perhaps a child could take on this role successfully if experienced in this way of working.

Framing and asking questions sensitively, using an appropriate tone of voice, talking in role, persuasion

Write a list of questions to ask Red Riding Hood

Role on the wall: collecting information about Red Riding Hood

Gather together the information that has been collected about the event in the form of a simple role on the wall. This involves drawing a figure to represent Red Riding Hood on a large sheet of paper and writing in the information that has been discussed (see Figure 2.2).

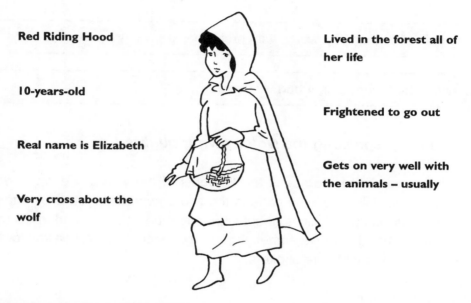

Red Riding Hood

10-years-old

Real name is Elizabeth

Very cross about the wolf

Lived in the forest all of her life

Frightened to go out

Gets on very well with the animals – usually

Figure 2.2 Role on the wall for RRH

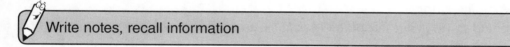

Write notes, recall information

You have been a very bad wolf!

Teacher's intentions

- To be able to give personal opinions;
- To consider feelings of others and alternative viewpoints.

Thought tunnel: what do we think about the wolf's behaviour?

Tell the children that they are going to be able to tell the wolf what they think of his behaviour. Give some examples in order to avoid inappropriate statements!

- *I think you should be ashamed of yourself.*
- *Why did you do it?*
- *I hope you'll be in prison for a long time.*

Children form two parallel lines facing into the path between the lines. Teacher in role as wolf walks down the path and each character has the opportunity to express his or her thoughts about him. The wolf cannot reply to the comments and questions and walks slowly along the path, looking miserable (see Figure 2.3).

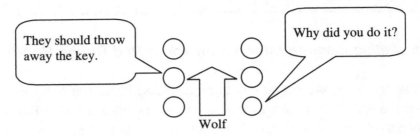

Figure 2.3 The thought tunnel

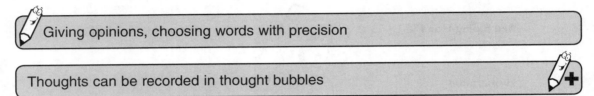

Giving opinions, choosing words with precision

Thoughts can be recorded in thought bubbles

Conscience alley: speaking the wolf's own thoughts

The children are now asked to speak the thoughts of the wolf as he walks down the corridor towards the police cell, the cage in the zoo or wherever you decide to put him after his crime! Discuss possibilities about what might be going around in his mind first so everyone feels that they have something to say. Teacher in role walks slowly along the corridor and his thoughts are spoken.

- *I wish I hadn't done it.*
- *I'm in big trouble.*
- *Still, I was really hungry.*
- *I wasn't going to do it but I couldn't resist. It was typical of that nosy woodcutter to barge in at the wrong moment.*
- *I'm sorry.*
- *How will my wife and seven cubs get on without me?*
- *I hope the judge is lenient.*

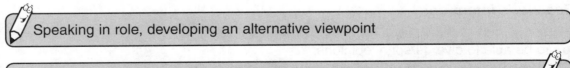

Speaking in role, developing an alternative viewpoint

Recording the wolf's thoughts in thought bubbles

Alternative activity

An alternative activity to the thought tunnel could be done with the children sitting in a square around the wolf to represent the walls of the prison cell, the bars of the cage or wherever you decide he is sitting. The teacher in role as wolf could pace around while the children speak his thoughts, as before (see Figure 2.4).

Figure 2.4 An alternative to a thought tunnel

Finding out more information

Teacher's intentions

- To deepen understanding of alternative viewpoints;
- To add detail to the story.

Interviewing: what do you know about the incident?

In pairs, the children are given the task of interviewing and being interviewed. The pairs could be:

- a local newspaper reporter interviewing Red Riding Hood's mother;
- a police constable interviewing the woodcutter;
- an animal behaviourist interviewing the wolf.

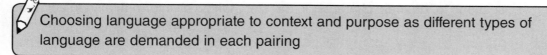

Choosing language appropriate to context and purpose as different types of language are demanded in each pairing

Key points could be recorded or a report written

Meeting and teacher in role: what should be done about the wolf's behaviour?

Tell the children that there is going to be a meeting arranged to discuss local problems. Children in role as villagers or woodland dwellers are invited to a meeting in the village hall or the clearing in the wood to discuss the incident at Granny's cottage and other important local issues. Ask the children to set up the space as if there was to be a formal meeting. Chairs can be used to form rows, otherwise sit on the floor.

Teacher takes on the role of an authority figure such as a mayor, vicar, neighbourhood watch coordinator or head teacher and welcomes everyone to the meeting. A pupil could take on this role successfully and perhaps be supported by one or two other children in minor lead roles. They would need to be carefully briefed.

There was a terrible incident in the wood last week and I know that many of you have said that you are worried that this might only be the start. Has anybody got anything that they want to say about the incident with the wolf or any other incidents that they know about?

Chair of the meeting invites comments and questions from the meeting.

At the end of this meeting tell the group that there is a visitor who would like to come and speak to them.

Teacher now takes the role of the wolf's wife. She has been to visit him. She is able to tell the meeting that the wolf is really sorry and that he was over-excited/just playing/was really hungry … and wants to be forgiven. He knows that he has done wrong but wishes that he could be given a second chance.

The children have to decide whether they will be able to forgive the wolf and if so what are their conditions. There is no right or wrong decision and it may be that there is no definitive decision made by the meeting. The wolf's wife can leave at any point to let the meeting consider what to do.

> Putting forward a point of view in a formal meeting situation using appropriate language

> Write minutes of the meeting
>
> Write rules for the wolf to follow if he is allowed to stay

What conclusions have we come to about the wolf?

Teacher's intentions

- To give reactions to the main character in the story taking all information in to account.

Statementing: sharing individual personal views about the wolf

Each member of the group, in role, has the opportunity to say what he or she thinks about the wolf now, after hearing different points of view by making another statement about him. This time, a chair is put into the middle of a circle (on which we imagine that the wolf is sitting). One at a time, the children come forward towards the chair and speak their thoughts about the story.

- *You were very naughty.*
- *I think you feel sorry now.*
- *Don't do it again.*
- *I don't think you are really sorry.*
- *Will the woods ever be safe again?*

> Speaking in role, choosing appropriate language

Writing the end of the story

Writing part of the story from the viewpoint of a chosen character

Writing a character study of the wolf or Red Riding Hood

Sculpting: the wolf at different stages throughout the story

This could be done in pairs or as a whole group. The teacher or a child is sculpted by the children to represent the wolf at given moments in the story. Choose three different points in the story such as the beginning, the moment of capture and in his cage or prison cell. These can be focused on to investigate the use of body posture and gesture to convey the feelings of characters. Depending on how brave or trusting you are, either follow instructions given by children to refine your position, or children can come forward and physically manipulate parts of your body until an agreed sculpture of the wolf is created.

- *At the beginning of the story, when he meets Red Riding Hood in the wood, how is he going to be feeling?*
- *How will he look to show that he is feeling happy and excited?*
- *Shall we see him standing or sitting?*
- *How will he stand then?*
- *What about his paws?*
- *Will his head be hanging down like this or up like this?*
- *What about the expression on his face?*
- *Is his back straight enough for this moment in the story?*

 Choosing words precisely, giving clear instructions

Writing a letter to the wolf in prison

Writing lists of words to describe the wolf at different times in the story

Retelling the story

Teacher's intentions

- To consolidate understanding of different key moments in the story;
- To deepen understanding of different characters.

Freeze frames, thought tapping and caption making: key moments in the story

Tell the children that they are going to tell the story in pictures, like the pictures in a storybook. They are going to make the pictures in the form of freeze frames. Ask the children to think about the key moments in the story.

In groups of three or four, children are given a specific moment in the story to show as a freeze frame. All of the children in the group will need to be involved in the picture so some may need to represent furniture or trees, or one may be designated to speak the caption (see below). The pictures could show:

- packing the basket of goodies for Granny;
- leaving home and setting off through the forest;
- meeting the wolf in the clearing in the wood;
- arriving at Granny's cottage;
- inside the wolf's tummy;
- the arrival of the woodcutter;
- the Police/RSPCA takes the wolf away;
- the wolf in prison/the zoo being visited by his family;
- Granny being visited by her friends;
- the woodcutter being given a bravery award by the mayor.

Children practise the freeze frames before showing them to the whole group.

Each group is asked to decide on a caption for their picture. What caption would go underneath this picture in a book?
    The groups then show the pictures in a random order and everyone else reads the picture to discover which moment is being shown. The captions are spoken out loud to accompany each picture. You can find out more about what is happening in the picture by thought tapping or speaking to any of the people in it.

- *What can you see in front of you?*
- *How are you feeling at this moment?*
- *What do you think will happen now?*
- *What are you saying at this moment?*
- *What do you think about the fact that a wolf has eaten you?*
- *Do you think it is wise to send a young girl out into the woods alone?*
- *What do you think your punishment will be for this crime?*
- *Describe your reaction to this event.*

Now ask the children to decide in which order the pictures would go if they were to be published in a book. Tell the children that you are going to use the pictures to retell the story and that at the right moment in the story each group will make the appropriate picture and read or speak the caption that goes with it.
    The freeze frame pictures are then put into the right order chronologically and shown again, with the teacher miming the turning over of pages in a large book to reveal each new picture and narrating a shortened version of the story to incorporate all of the pictures. For example, mime holding a large book and reading the title:

The story of Little Red Riding Hood ... [mime reading the first page]. *Once upon a time there was a little girl who had to visit her sick Granny who lived on the other side of the wood. The girl helped her mother to pack a basket of goodies to take with her.*

Group 1 makes a still image of the basket being packed and one person speaks the caption: *Granny will love all of these things.* After the image has been shown the group sits down to watch the others.

Note that this activity has a real feeling of ritual. There is definite tension created here as the children strive to get their image right and a real sense of whole class cooperation is built up. It can be practised and refined and possibly performed as a piece for an assembly or school play.

Recalling, listing

Expressing feelings, answering questions, literal, inferential and evaluative comprehension

Make a list of key moments in chronological order or fill in a simple storyboard

Captions could be written on paper and revealed at an appropriate moment

Reflection: what have we learned?

It is important that the wider implications of the story are discussed.

- *Why did the wolf behave as he did?*
- *Was the reaction of the villagers appropriate?*
- *What did the main characters learn?*
- *What have we learned about human nature through doing this drama?*

Chapter 3
Rubbish in the River

Learning objectives

- To understand path of rivers;
- High order reading skills;
- Journalistic writing.

Themes

- Rubbish and environmental care;
- Journalists on an environmental story.

Resources

- Six sheets or more of sugar paper prepared with a river drawing (see Figure 3.2).

Time

- One hour.

Things have gone from bad to worse in our town

Teacher's intentions

- To establish the context of the drama;
- To introduce the roles of journalists.

Teacher in role and discussion: journalists are addressed by the editor

Teacher explains to the class that in the drama they are going to have a big job to do as journalists of a local newspaper called *The Abington Herald*. As top journalists they have all been called to a meeting with the editor of the paper. Teacher plays the role of Ed, the editor.

Thanks very much for coming to this meeting. I need to have you on this new job because you are the best. This story will run and run. Let me explain.

As you will know, Charlestown has long been known as one of the finest and prettiest towns in the country. Long have the people of Charlestown been proud of their scenic river and rarely has a community used its river so fully. The landscapes around the river are beautiful and the care of these areas has continued to be a top priority for the town council. It seems that something terrible has happened, but I haven't been given details. Instead I have been asked to send my top journalists to speak to a town councillor. Please go and find out all you can.

Out of role, children share their understanding of what they have been told.

● *Who are you? What is your reputation as journalists in this drama?*
● *What is the task you are being set?*
● *Where are you to go?*
● *Who are you to interview?*
● *What is a town councillor?*
● *Where might you meet the councillor?*
● *What should you ask the councillor?*

 Listening for key points, summarizing information

Write a list of questions to ask

Teacher in role in a meeting: the journalists meet the councillor

Invite the children to plan how they imagine the room would be set out for the meeting between journalists and the town councillor. Teacher plays the councillor, who is very worried and serious. You may decide to have other aspects such as being friendly or a bit short tempered.

The journalists ask questions and the councillor reveals the following:

● *The town has been proud of its beauty;*
● *Regent's River had always given such pleasure;*
● *Some months ago people began to see bits of rubbish in the river;*
● *More recently it has become worse, with cans and bottles and even cereal packets;*
● *People no longer swim or fish in the river;*
● *No one has seen people dropping litter into the river, and why would this suddenly start happening?*
● *Please could you speak to people and see how they are suffering and make a splash in the press to raise attention to our problem. I expect there are lots of nonsense stories going around as they do when extraordinary things happen. We are desperate for help.*

Interviewing: journalists seek their story

Journalists are asked to prepare questions in groups that they could ask the people of the town about the problem, e.g.

- *How is it affecting your life?*
- *Who do you think is doing this?*
- *What was the town like before?*

In pairs, A as journalist and B as townsperson, an interview is carried out. If appropriate, swap roles around so B becomes the interviewee and A the journalist.

Whole-group improvisation: devising headlines

In fours, as journalists, share the responses gained and consider suitable headlines.

Consider examples of attention-grabbing newspaper headlines and discuss what it is about them that makes us wish to read on. Perhaps you can look at the jokes and puns in headlines and the seriousness of others.

Journalists prepare and write headlines to attract attention to the problem, through perhaps humour, or alarmist effect.

> Talking in role

> Writing headlines, using ICT where appropriate. Consider different layouts
>
> Collect headlines from the week's newspapers.

Investigating the problem

Teacher's intentions

- To introduce idea of investigative journalism;
- To practise tactful and searching questions;
- To introduce the idea of competition in newspapers.

Meeting: teacher in role sets a challenge for the journalists

Take the role of the editor, Ed, to talk about the headlines the journalists are proposing. Thank them for their work on these and explain that sub-writers will now produce articles on their interview data. The journalists now have a more important role.

- The problem needs to be investigated;
- The best story to be in the *Herald* would be the one that finds out who or what is to blame for the litter problem;
- The worst scenario would be the rival paper, *The Morning Post*, printing that story;
- Something strange has happened. An envelope has been found on the doorstep of the building'
- It is are chopped-up words, and perhaps they might say something about the problem;
- Please do your best to work out what is meant and investigate until you have the answer, so we beat *The Morning Post*!

Whole-group improvisation: group problem solving

Divide the class into six groups. Each is given an envelope with paper fragments, which each provide a different clue. See Figure 3.1. Each group has a clue written on a shape, so that they have to place the pieces into the right places to reveal the lines which make up the clue. The shapes have the clues clearly written on. They are then cut up according to how much of a challenge you wish to give different groups.

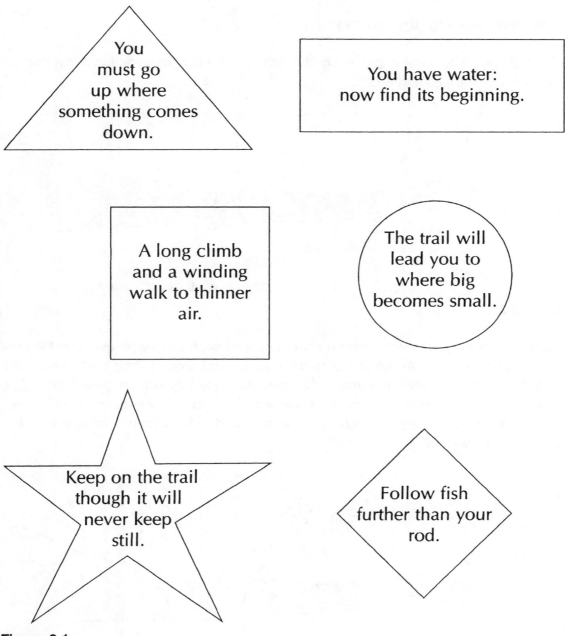

Figure 3.1

The groups discuss what they could mean.

The teacher as Ed could bring them together to see how some clues help others understand their clues. They determine that they must follow the river into the mountains.

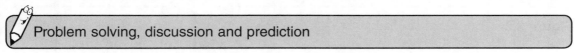

Problem solving, discussion and prediction

Journey to solve the problem

Teacher's intentions

- To present a group story;
- To consider how to create suspense in storytelling.

Collective drawing: the journey

Bring out sheets of sugar paper, each of which has already got a section of river drawn across it, gradually getting wider.

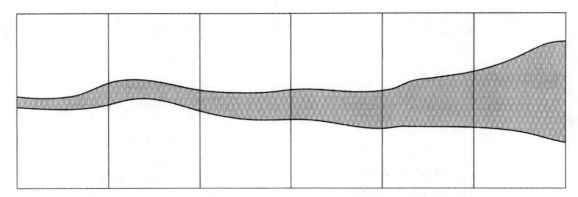

Figure 3.2

Children work in groups, each with a sheet of paper each and some coloured felt pen/ wax crayons. They are asked to create the environment around 'their' part of the river, highlighting anything that may make the journalists' journey difficult (see Figure 3.3). They may include anything – swampy ground, high rocks, wolves, snakes, broken bridges. You may choose to teach map symbols and ask for them to use these, e.g. contour lines, swamps.

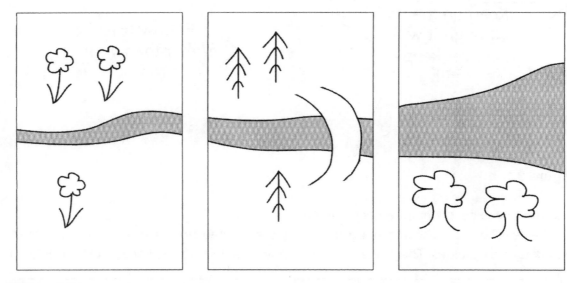

Figure 3.3

Storytelling: what happened on the journey?

Each group then prepares a story presentation to describe how the journalists coped with the journey at their part of the river. They can take turns and/or share some parts of the story. They may have some disasters on the way! They must consider how to tell their story in a way that will create interest and suspense.

- When should they vary the speed of the storytelling?
- Which parts should be spoken loudly and which quietly?
- Where should there be pauses to build anticipation or to emphasize a point?

Finally, all groups join their sections of the river together and in order starting from the widest part where the town lies, the stories of the journey are told.

Write a piece of descriptive writing of the journey for *The Abington Herald*

Write/draw a key for the map using symbols

Narration and discussion with teacher in role: meeting the 'problem'

As the last group finishes, pick up the story:

Eventually they got high up the mountain where their trail, the river, had become a stream. They were amazed to see a dustbin bag beside the stream and near it a small house. What a place to have a house! So high! It was certainly the only building for miles. The journalists discussed what they thought was going on and what they should ask the lady they could see in the window of the house.

They discuss the sort of approach they should take to the complete stranger and the questions they could pose. They must consider that they want to get to the bottom of the river's problem, to be sure they get all the information they can so that their paper has the big front page solving the town's mystery.

Explain that when you sit down you will be in role as the lady and the journalists can approach. A doorway could be agreed and perhaps a way they will attract her attention.

The lady is warm and friendly, welcoming her visitors. She explains that she rarely sees anyone up on the mountain and certainly not such a crowd. Have they come far? Would they like tea?

Give information only if the journalists ask in a way that makes the lady want to share her story. She is completely oblivious of causing anyone a problem. She has recently moved from a city where she used to put her bin bags out on to the pavement and a lorry used to come and take them away.

Here I just put my rubbish into my beautiful, fast-flowing stream and it is taken away. Then my stream is beautifully clear.

When the journalists explain that it is spoiling the river of their town, she is confused. It can't be so, because they talk about a big river. She puts her rubbish into a little stream.

Also, they live a long way away from here, so it can't be her rubbish. She has never considered where the rubbish has gone, somehow assuming it just disappeared. As the truth dawns on her she asks about the river, what they used to use it for and what it is like now.

You will decide how to react to the information by the way that the journalists speak to you. You may be very apologetic when you understand the situation and offer to return to the town with them and help them to clean up the river. Or you may tell them to get out of your house and mind their own business.

 Putting forward and argument, asking questions

 Taking notes

Hold the front page!

Teacher's intentions

- To create newspaper articles;
- To consider bias and different viewpoints.

Whole-group improvisation: planning and writing articles

Teacher in role as Ed leads a discussion about what the journalists might want their readers to think and feel when they read the newspaper articles about the discovery of the problem. Discuss what sort of language would help them to create that response. Some may wish to show off the journalists' achievement; others may wish to present the lady as a villain or as a reformed character. Discussion should include consideration of bias in texts.

Journalists work in pairs or small groups to draft articles.

Reflection: what have we learned?

Discuss the implications of portraying the lady at the centre of this story in different ways. Was she bad or just misguided? Do journalists have the right to be critical and judgemental or should they just state the facts? What sort of effect might different headlines have on the readers?

Perhaps look at some of the articles written by the journalists about this story and identify which words have been used to show bias.

 Discussion and developing and argument

 Write or compare two articles from two different standpoints

Chapter 4
Romans in Britain

The children in role as time travellers discover details of the Roman attack on Anglesey in AD 60. The all-powerful 'Great Mistress of Time' has a mission for the new team of travellers. They must go into the past and report on what they discover. They meet people from the past and get involved in past events, learning about the Roman occupation and the Britons' various responses to it. The children move between their time travelling roles in the present and different roles in the past. They must therefore address the situation from the point of view of the Romans and of the Britons, as well as that of observers in the present.

Learning objectives

- To learn about the Romans in Britain;
- To understand conflicting interests and different world views, considering different viewpoints and cultural differences;
- To adapt speech for a range of different purposes;
- To take up and sustain different roles, adapting them to suit the situation;
- To think about the lives of people living in other places and times, and people with different values and customs.

Themes

- Romans in Britain;
- Historical interpretation;
- Recognizing difference and challenging stereotypes.

Resources

- Felt pens, large sheets of paper;
- Time travel task provided (see Figure 4.1).

Time

- This work will take most groups between two and a half and three hours.

Notes

This time machine structure, with its opportunity to give much information and to critically consider events, can be used for other historical contexts. You could take the class to Victorian Britain, for example. You may wish to do only the first meeting with Marcus the Roman soldier. Historical information required for the drama is provided at the end of the chapter.

Sounds can enhance the atmosphere, e.g. the *Dr Who* theme could be used with the time tunnel.

Let's talk about time travel stories

Teacher's intentions

- To establish the idea of being time travellers;
- To set up the time travellers' task.

Discussion: what do we know?

Introduce the session by leading a general discussion about familiar books, television programmes and films about time travel.

- *Which have you read/seen?*
- *How does Dr Who move in time?*
- *What makes the films or books convincing?*
- *Do they take people forward or back in time?*

 Sharing ideas; relevant contributions

Defining space and setting the scene: introduction to the time tunnel

Tell the class that they are going to be involved in a drama about time travellers. Arrange the class in a circle of chairs and give the following outline:

When you are sitting on your chairs, you are in role as time travellers in the present day. However, everything that takes place in the centre of the circle is taking place in the time tunnel, and therefore in the past or future. It is through the time tunnel that moments of other times can be viewed.

We are all in the drama when I am inside our circle of chairs, but when I step behind my chair, it is the sign that I am out of role and will speak to you as your teacher.

Are you ready for the time travel drama?

Teacher in role and ritual: introducing the missions set by the Great Mistress of Time

Take the role of the Time Travel Controller, who shows a deep reverence for the Great Mistress of Time, in charge of the time machine. She is never seen, but her requests and comments are passed to the time travellers through you, the controller.

Welcome everyone and explain that before they are permitted to hear any details of the time machine missions they are required by the Great Mistress of Time to swear an oath. They must stand and raise their right hand.

Raise your right arm, with palm facing down, hand straight towards the centre of the circle. This should be done as though it is of crucial importance with a serious expression. When all the children have their right hands out, ask them to repeat each phrase together after you:

I swear
to keep the secrets
of the time machine.

Ask the children to be seated. Introduce the first task:

A little while ago, the Great Mistress of Time programmed the time machine for North Wales AD 60. She observed a young man talking to himself. What she saw made her feel very concerned and so she would like you to find out more for her. She has asked that I read you her account of what she saw.

This is provided in Figure 4.1. It looks better if you read it from a photocopied sheet rather than from this book. It could be displayed on screen.

> Modelling an appropriate tone and register of voice for the context

First mission: meeting the Roman soldier

Teacher's intentions

- To teach about the Romans in Britain;
- To create one perspective on Roman occupation.

Read aloud as the Controller:

AD 60   North Wales

I saw a man weeping. He looked young, strong and healthy. He was quite alone.

There were strange objects beside him, but I couldn't make out what they were. Something looked sharp. His clothes were strange – made of metal, I think.
I wondered if he was uncomfortable in the outfit.

He was muttering but I couldn't make out what he said. I'm sure I heard, between the sobs,
'Numbers against magic'.
I wonder what he meant.
He also said,
'So far, too far', about something.

Figure 4.1 The account from the Great Mistress of Time

Teacher in role discussion: deconstructing the text

Teacher in role leads time travellers in a discussion of the text. What do we know? What do we want to find out?

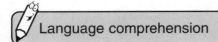

Language comprehension

Teacher in role: introducing the first mission

Time travellers, it is the request of the Great Mistress of Time that we programme the machine to North Wales AD 60 and find this young man. We will then have to ask him questions to find out as much as we can about him and his life. What sort of questions might we ask?

Ask the children to frame questions in time travel pairs first. Expect questions such as:

- *What is your name?*
- *Why are you crying?*
- *How old are you?*
- *What are the sharp things beside you?*
- *Why are you wearing such odd clothes?*

Ask them if they are ready for their mission, reminding them that the Mistress will want a very full report.

Deduction from what has been heard, framing questions

Annotate the 'transcript' of the account, highlighting the things we know and things we want to find out with different coloured pens. This could be done using ICT

Whole-group improvisation: going back to Wales AD 60

Teacher in role stands up as the time traveller in serious mode. Mime turning dials and pushing buttons as you say the year, AD 60, and place, North Wales.

I wish you well. I am not permitted to accompany you on this, your first mission. I will programme the machine and soon a vision of this young man in the past will appear before your eyes ... in the tunnel of time.

Find out all you can. The Great Mistress of Time needs to know everything.

Turn slowly in circles, moving into the centre of the circle. Sit down in the middle to become Marcus, a young Roman soldier, wiping his eyes. Marcus is innocent and friendly. He means well and will gain the children's affection. He is excited about the weapons, yet worried about their consequences. He believes that he is doing what is right. The class as time travellers question Marcus, who is happy to have someone to speak to. Here an enormous amount of information can be given. Details can be found in background information at the end of this chapter.

Marcus shows off his two javelins and short sword, proud that it is not long and unwieldy like the Britons' swords. He asks them not to be afraid when he shows them his helmet on his head, because it is designed to frighten off the enemy. He explains how he has been trained to march, to use his shield, and in how the Britons fight.

In response to questions about his tears, he may deny them at first. His fear is of the battle he is forced to fight the next day. He believes that the Druids are magic and may therefore overwhelm even the best-trained soldiers. He tells that the Druids are evil, since they make human sacrifices in the forest. The Britons have not been grateful for all that the Romans have brought to Britain. They didn't have roads or cities before, and in return they are fighting! Some have been very nice and made friends with Roman generals, but not the Druids on Anglesey. Marcus misses his family. He is only fourteen years old. He is proud of being a soldier, but is afraid, and needs reassurance that he will be all right. Finally, he explains that he must get back to the camp or he will be missed by his best friend, Phillipos.

Stand and turn slowly in circles moving back towards the Time Travel Controller's chair. Sit on it and then look up as the Time Travel Controller.

Asking questions to derive information

Using language for a particular purpose, using an appropriate voice and wording to demonstrate empathy

Write a report of the mission to begin creating a log of what has been discovered

Reporting back on the findings

Teacher's intentions

- To recall the new information they have heard;
- To introduce the idea of perspective, as well as fact.

Role on the wall: recording the information gained on the mission

As Time Travel Controller, ask the time travellers if they saw anyone on their mission. What did they find out?

The time travellers are introduced to the way that all missions in the time tunnel are recorded. A large sheet of paper is spread on the floor. Draw a stick figure to represent Marcus and write around it as much information provided by Marcus as the children can remember. Write the information in note form as it is offered by the children. It can be about the Romans' fighting techniques, the Druids and Marcus himself. You could write details of Britons and Romans, such as their different weaponry, in different colours.

His name is Marcus.
He is frightened of the Druids.
The Romans all carry two javelins each.

You, as the time traveller, were not on the mission with the children, so you can use the role to clarify details, thus:

- *Did he tell you the name of the island the Druids were on?*
- *What did his helmet look like?*
- *What were the sharp things?*

You can also challenge the information:

● *Did he ever actually see the Druids doing magic?*
● *Did he think that the Britons wanted new roads?*

Avoid correcting information (perhaps the number of javelins Marcus carried), because in the drama, you weren't there! Usually the children correct one another at this stage; otherwise you can give correct information later in the drama.

When all the information they have is noted on the paper, congratulate the team on their first mission.

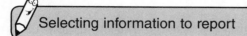 Selecting information to report

Charts and maps depicting the journey Marcus had taken from Rome to Anglesey

Research life in Rome – could be presented to the Controller for the files of the Great Mistress of Time

MARCUS

Druids on foot

Wealthy Britons have small chariots

Marcus aged 14

Has two Javelins

Marcus afraid of the Druids

Figure 4.2 Marcus

Roman soldiers prepare for battle

Teacher's intentions

- To correct any misunderstandings already formed;
- To imagine being in a Roman soldier's shoes.

Whole-group improvisation and teacher in role: the Roman soldiers are briefed before battle

Move outside the circle of chairs and, speaking as teacher, explain that the children will soon need to become people in the past for the next part of the drama.

Back inside the circle, the Time Travel Controller passes on the Mistress's interest in their work and in the life of Marcus. They are now to travel back in time to the same place, but this time to the following morning to see what happened next.

They are to be introduced to the 'freeze control' facility of the time machine, which stops any given moment in time so that it can be examined.

As I programme the time machine [mime turning dials as before], an image will appear. I can see a scene as the swirling mists clear. It is early morning. I can see a cold grey sea [point]. On the beach there are rows of soldiers standing very upright, in silence. They stand in rows facing the sea.

Indicate, by gesturing to the children, that they are to become the soldiers.

They must be waiting for something very important ... Oh yes, there is a general coming to speak to them!

Step in front of the rows and address the soldiers as their general. Now is the opportunity to correct any misinformation from the first mission. Perhaps they didn't catch the name of the island, for example. Through this role you can also give additional information. Tell them:

- *We don't know what to expect on the Isle of Anglesey;*
- *The Druids must be destroyed because they have resisted the Romans;*
- *The Druids still make human sacrifices, which Romans stopped long ago;*
- *To remember all their training – javelins thrown only on command, shields above them, close together to protect from arrows and spears, and so on;*
- *They will cross the Menai Straits to Anglesey in flat-bottomed boats;*
- *Mounted soldiers will swim across with their horses;*
- *Druids must be killed to make Britain a safer place;*
- *The wood on Anglesey must be cut down because the Druids believe it is sacred and make their sacrifices there.*

Ask if the soldiers have any questions.

Freeze frame and thought tap: how are the soldiers feeling?

Return to the edge of the circle and explain that you are going to turn on the freeze control now, which will freeze this moment in time.

Walking around the still image of soldiers, you wonder what they are thinking. A new device on the time machine can enable you to tap soldiers on the shoulder and they speak aloud their thoughts. Provide some examples.

Perhaps one is thinking, 'I am afraid,' or 'Are the Druids really magic?' or maybe, 'I wish I was at home.'

Tap individuals and hear the thoughts. You may need to repeat each one so that they are all heard.

Finally, return to your position as Time Travel Controller.

The image is slowly and silently fading away.

Gesture to the children to return to their time travel seats.

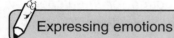 Expressing emotions

Write a diary entry or a letter home in role as one of the soldiers, including thoughts and feelings

Role on the wall: adding information

A report must be made of the second mission for the Great Mistress of Time. Revisit the Marcus role on the wall and add new information or correct anything that was recorded wrongly. Alternatively, you could use a new sheet for the second mission. This time you can comment on what was observed because you were watching events through the time tunnel, too.

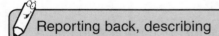 Reporting back, describing

Draw the weapons carried by the Roman foot soldier, e.g. short sword. Annotate with the specifications and advantages

Research Roman Soldiers

Meanwhile, the Druids prepare on Anglesey

Teacher's intentions

● To introduce another perspective.

Teacher in role: introducing a new mission

The time travellers are told that the Great Mistress of Time is curious to know how the other side is preparing on Anglesey. Their next mission will take them over the Menai Straits to see how the Britons are preparing. A full report will again be requested.

The controls are set. Looking into the time tunnel (the centre of the circle), describe the vision revealed:

There are crowds of people sitting down on the ground, all facing the sea. [Gesture for the children to sit down in role as the Britons.] *The women are all clad in black and the Druid priests are looking fearfully out to sea and to the heavens. It's a cold day and many are hugging themselves to keep warm. No one speaks. At last someone gets to his feet. He is an old man with a wise though anxious face. All turn with respect to listen to him.*

Stand and give the gist or read the old Druid's speech:

We know the gods are on our side. The gods know that this is our land. These intruders have no right to walk on our land, no right to shed our blood, no right to interfere with our sacred ways. All of us here know how they have persuaded many Britons, with money and honours, to lay down their swords.

I am proud that I am here with Britons who will not be bought or threatened by Roman invaders. We wish to keep our soil for those of future generations. We do not wish to have their new cities – we like things as they were.

Let us be true to ourselves and the gods and fight with all our might. We will wait here until they come, then run at them with swords, clubs and anything we have, shouting curses upon those who wish to destroy what means so much to us.

Thank you. I honour you for your courage.

Step outside the chairs to give instructions as teacher. Clarify what has been heard so far.

 Identify gist of what is heard, give main points

Overheard conversations: how do the Britons feel?

Explain that the Britons talked, as they waited, about all that had been said and about their hopes and fears. Ask the children to chat with those near them in threes or fours as though they are the Britons. When you clap your hands it is the freeze control and they must remain still. You will then wander about the groups. When you stand by a group, they must continue their conversation until you move on.

When snippets of each conversation have been heard, end the mission by describing the image slowly disappearing and gesturing to the children to return to their seats.

 Speaking in role, re-presenting ideas in a different way (written to spoken)

Script short Druid conversations

Research Anglesey

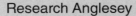

Role on the wall

Draw up a new report on a sheet of paper with the outline shape of an island.

- *What did you see happening on Anglesey?*
- *Did they look ready for the battle?*
- *Why were they fighting against good people, anyway?*
- *Are they misunderstood by the Romans?*
- *What did they talk about?*
- *Were they like you thought they would be?*

 Responding to the views of others, taking account of what they have said

Photographs of the battle and conclusions

Teacher's intentions

- To provide a dramatic activity that reinforces the learning on weaponry and fighting methods;
- To consider different perspectives and debate the implications in the context of Roman Britain.

Small group freeze frames and mime: the battle

The Time Travel Controller informs the time travellers that the Great Mistress of Time is very impressed by their work and asks if they will complete one final mission. She wants them to watch the battle and take photographs for her of what they see.

As teacher, outside the circle of chairs, explain that in groups of three or four they should create two photographs showing moments of the battle. They must use their new knowledge of how the Romans and Britons fight so that it is clear who is fighting on which side.

As Time Travel Controller, invite each group in turn to show the photographs they have taken. These can be discussed. Then ask for all the photos to be placed in the centre to create a big battle scene.

As teacher, outside the circle, explain that you will narrate the battle story and if the children are tapped on the shoulder, they must silently fall to the floor as dead.

Walk slowly between the children's photos as you narrate the battle. Use your voice to create a tense atmosphere as you explain the Romans' initial fear at the sight of the Druids, then describe the huge numbers of well-equipped, trained soldiers moving in on the untrained, ill-equipped Britons. As you move, gradually touch the shoulders of more Britons than Romans to signify deaths. Describe the fighting, the Britons' long swords and the sounds of anguish and weeping that filled the air.

After destroying most of the Britons, the order was given to cut down the sacred wood.

Mime chopping down trees and then, looking at the children, some remaining in fighting positions and others dead, describe the image of the past battle fading, and return to time travel seats.

 Listening and responding

Write a report or a description of the battle

Reflection: what have we learned?

The Time Travel Controller congratulates the time travellers. Their work has intrigued, fascinated and bewildered the Great Mistress of Time. She would be very grateful if they would consider some questions:

- *If you had been alive in AD 60, who would you rather have been?*
- *What exactly were the different views?*
- *Who do you think should have won the battle?*
- *Who do you think was right?*
- *Should the Romans have been in Britain?*
- *Did you feel sympathy for either side? Both?*
- *Living in the present, do you think the country is better or worse for having had the Roman invasion?*

The children are thanked for their work and assured that they are the best team of time travellers ever to take a mission in the time machine.

 Qualification and justification of views after listening to others

Summarizing main points

Reason and argument

Under two columns, Fact and Fiction, list what happened in their drama. For example, in AD 60 the Romans mounted an attack on Anglesey = Fact; a boy called Marcus was afraid of fighting = Fiction. This may raise some interesting discussion about evidence and viewpoint

Presentation of discoveries made through time tunnel

Background information

Marcus

Marcus is in the Roman army. He is fourteen years old. He was very sorry to leave his family in Rome, but proud to march with the army as his brothers and father did.

'So far, too far' refers to the long distance he has travelled from warm, blue-skied Rome to cold, grey Britain. There are things he misses about home. It was a long, tiring march to get here.

Marcus has crept from the soldiers' tent at night to be alone. He is embarrassed by his tears and may pretend that he hasn't been crying. He is afraid because General Suetonius is to give the command tomorrow morning. They must cross the Menai Straits to invade Anglesey.

'Numbers against magic' refers to the Roman soldiers' belief that the Druid priests, who had gathered in Anglesey, had magic powers. Marcus is unsure whether the highly trained, vast armies of Rome can outdo the magic he believes the Britons have on their side. He may ask the time travellers if they believe in magic and if they think he will be okay.

Roman weaponry

A short sword: Marcus laughs at the swords of the Britons, which are long and unwieldy. He has been trained to use the short sword, which enables precision. (He hasn't actually killed before and may be a bit anxious about the thought of it. A short sword means being very close to the victim.)

Two javelins: the soldiers may only throw their javelins on command. The enemy is showered twice by volleys of javelins. The Britons throw spears that could be hurled back at them by their enemy. The Romans' superior design ensured no Romans could be killed by their own weapons: the head of the javelin broke off on impact. Marcus will be proud of this and can demonstrate how a javelin is thrown.

Rectangular, curved shield: the shields are designed so that the soldiers can stand close to one another holding their shields tilted in front of them, protecting themselves to the front and above. The shields touch edges so that the arrows and spears of the Britons hit the shields and cannot harm the soldiers. Marcus may 'show' the large projection in the centre of his shield. It is used to batter enemy soldiers. It looks pretty lethal.

Helmet: the Roman helmet makes Marcus feel better. It is so large that the enemy will think that he is bigger than he really is. They will then be frightened of him. He mimes putting the helmet on, asking the time travellers not to be afraid! He strokes the large imagined plume explaining that it gives height. He strokes his hand down his cheeks to show them where the pieces of metal come down to protect his face. There is also curved metal at the back of the neck.

Armour: the Roman design consists of narrow strips of metal running horizontally across the body. The metal strips are joined at the top and bottom by tiny metal rings. The soldiers can therefore move about very easily and comfortably, and their armour is not as heavy as solid plate armour.

Britons in battle

Marcus scorns the untrained methods of the Britons. (His only fear is of magic.) The wealthier Britons have two-horse chariots on which they ride across the front of the Romans to throw their spears. Britons also use long swords, bows and arrows, and slings and stones. Some have armour that restricts their movements and must have been heavy to wear. Shields were a variety of shapes and sizes, often with patterns or pictures.

A Roman view of Britons

Marcus knows that some Britons have been 'sensible' and appreciative of what the Romans have done for Britain – the towns and roads, for example. He believes that they are lucky to be learning Latin and Roman, 'civilized' ways. It is a mystery to him why other Britons have been so rebellious and unappreciative. Marcus has heard of a crazy woman called Boudicca, whose father was a friend to the Romans. She is now stirring up trouble in East Anglia, and Marcus will have to march over there when they have sorted out the Druids on Anglesey.

The Druids seem a strange lot to Marcus. They seem to know a lot about nature, the seasons and crops. He is disgusted because he has heard that there is a wood that is sacred to the Druids on Anglesey. There they make human sacrifices to their gods. (The Romans had given up human sacrifices at this time.) The Druids have consistently resisted the Romans and have continually been defeated. They have fled to or gathered in Anglesey. Marcus may have heard rumours that there is good corn or even gold under the ground on Anglesey, but understands that the invasion is to put a stop to these people who have caused the Romans such trouble, once and for all.

Chapter 5
Building the Pyramid

An ancient Egyptian architect has a very important meeting planned with the Pharaoh. Unfortunately, he is sick and unable to go. He needs the help of the children to find out details of the new building the Pharaoh wants him to construct. They need to consider what the architect would need to know, such as the size, the materials and the purpose of the building. Once this information has been reported back to the architect, the children create the images depicting farming scenes that are painted on the pyramid walls. Finally, they meet the farmers who are recruited to build the pyramid and discover the conditions under which they worked.

Learning objectives

- To learn about life in Ancient Egypt;
- To speak with confidence in a range of different contexts;
- To ask questions to gather information;
- To recall details and report back information.

Themes

- Ancient Egypt
- Design: buildings and their purposes.

Resources

- Pyramid pictures (see Figures 5.1, 5.2, 5.3);
- Embalming instructions (see activity 4).
- Large sheets of paper and marker pens.

Time

- This work will take a minimum of two hours but could take up to three.

Notes

- The teacher needs to prepare by reading the historical information provided. The drama was inspired by David Macauley's *Pyramid* (1976), published by Collins,

London. You may choose to do only the first meeting of the children and the Pharaoh. This provides the children with an enormous amount of information and can be followed by work on design plans or further historical study.

Providing historical context

Teacher's intentions

- To give a sense of different eras;
- To provide factual information about pyramids and how they were built.

Game

Explain that the drama is about a time far in the past: the times of Ancient Egypt, which began around 5000 years ago and stretched until around 300 BC. The following game helps to imagine a time long ago.

Standing in a large circle, the children each think of an object. In turn, they enter the circle announcing the object, for example, a kettle. The children must then call 'yes' or 'no' depending on whether they think the object would have been around in Ancient Egypt. So, kettle would obviously get a call of 'no', while pots, tools and clothes would all get a 'yes'.

 Listening and responding

 Draw time lines and research objects that might be appropriate for the periods

Discussion: what can we tell from this picture?

Look at the picture in Figure 5.1 and talk with the children about it.

- *Who do you think is more important? Why?*
- *What are the differences between the two figures?*
- *What has the sitting figure got on his head?*
- *Why might they be wearing so little?*
- *What is a pharaoh?*

Finally, tell the children that in their story the standing figure is Mahnud Hotep, who is a very good and hardworking architect, and the seated figure is his Pharaoh, who has told Mahnud that he wants a new building built in his kingdom of Egypt.

Figure 5.1 The meeting

Mahnud the architect needs help with an important job

Teacher's intentions

- To brief the children about their meeting with the Pharaoh;
- To frame questions to ask the Pharaoh.

Whole-group improvisation: planning a meeting with the Pharaoh

In this activity the teacher and children take on no distinct roles but they are clearly not themselves, because they speak as though they are in Ancient Egypt.

Explain to the children that Mahnud has some very bad luck. He is sick and he is meant to have a meeting with the Pharaoh today to talk about the new building. He is too ill to go, but is terrified that he may lose the work if he fails to take the details from the Pharaoh. He needs the job to support his family and this job would secure him work for some time.

He wonders if the children would be prepared to go to the Pharaoh in his place to find out all they can about what sort of building the Pharaoh wants built. Mahnud would be very grateful to them. He really needs their help. (If they are reluctant, you could offer a share of the finances! We don't usually find it necessary.)

Once they have agreed to go, explain that you don't know what sort of things they need to ask about the building. Mahnud will obviously need very detailed information. Can they think of what they will need to find out? Some examples children give and possible teacher responses are shown below:

What is it to be made of?
I don't know. Maybe he wants a wooden building.

What does he want to use it for?
Good point. It could be for parties!

Where does he want it?
I hadn't thought of that! Mahnud will need to know.

When does it need to be built?
Of course! Mahnud may not have much time.

How much will he pay?
He will certainly want to know that!

How big does he want it?
Good question. He may want a little cosy place.

What will it look like?
Yes! We need to ask that. Could be orange towers ...

Tell them to find out all they can, and remind them to be polite to the Pharaoh! You can hear him coming!

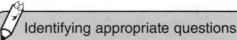
Identifying appropriate questions

Research the location of Egypt on the internet

Research pharaohs

Meeting the Pharaoh

Teacher's intentions

● For children to question the Pharaoh and gather useful information.

Whole-group improvisation: speaking to the Pharaoh

Teacher in role as the Pharaoh enters with great dignity. You may hold your hands up, palms out, looking at the children before you are seated. Though not authentic, this adds a bit of ritual to the drama. Sit with your feet square in front of you, straight back, and hands flat on each knee.

The children will then ask their teacher (who is in role as Pharaoh) for all the information that you want them to learn about pyramids! They will want to know all that you want to teach them. They want to know for Mahnud, rather than because it is on the curriculum, but the effect is the same: children learn all you can tell them about pyramids!

Make the children work for the information, not giving all the details at once. We have enjoyed playing quite a haughty pharaoh who wants his building slightly higher than his father's! We have also played pharaohs who really don't like to be bothered with these tedious details, but, well, will give them some of his precious time.

Ideas for answers to the most obvious questions are provided here:

What is it to be made of?
Stone. Homes for our short lives on earth may be of mud, but for the eternal afterlife, the building must last. Stone it must be. It can be shipped from the quarry down the Nile. About 50,000 men will be needed to transport the stone from the quarry to the site. [Boats and sledges were used to move the stone when there were no wheels.]

What do you want to use it for?
For my body to rest. There my 'ba', soul, will rest beside my mummified body and my 'ka', spirit, will travel between my body on earth and the other world. There must be a secret passageway for my 'ka' to leave and enter. It must be secret. No one must find the way in.

Where do you want it?
On the west bank of the Nile, for there the sun sets, beginning its nightly journey into the other world. I will be nearer Ra, the sun god, if the building is there.

When does it need to be built?
I do not know when I will require this building. But you have no time to waste since just to prepare the site and establish the foundations will take about seven years.

How much will you pay?
Mahnud will be well paid. The farmers who will be carrying out the hard labour will be paid in food and clothes. They will be pleased for this since they cannot farm between July and November when the Nile floods.

How big do you want it?
Good question: 146 metres, please.

What will it look like?

I wish it to be a perfect pyramid so that from above it appears as four rays of the sun protecting me. This will link me to Ra, the god of the sun.

Macauley's book provides interesting detail, such as the stones having to be all the same size exactly, and each group of twenty working on the cutting of one stone would have their own mark on the stone. In this way, punishment could be given for any stone not perfectly cut.

 Using a formal speech register

 Groups research different aspects e.g. farming, gods and the Nile, and present their findings.

Research photographs of pyramids and label features

Reporting back to Mahnud

Teacher's intentions

- To use the newly acquired information;
- To support the new learning and check it has been understood.

Children now need to assimilate and use the newly acquired information. Here are three possibilities. If you want to assess individual children's level of knowledge, activity (c) may be most appropriate.

(a) By whole-group improvisation

You may want to check out how much information the children have picked up. Asking them to tell Mahnud is our favourite way. As Mahnud, you can ask about particular things that you need to know to jog their memories. You must not imply that you were there! Why does he want it that shape?

 Selecting appropriate details and clearly expressing them

(b) By small group planning

Another possibility is to ask small groups to prepare plans and notes of information on large sheets of paper. They then present the brief to Mahnud.

 Presentation

(c) With an individual writing task

Alternatively, children could individually write a report for Mahnud, giving him the details he requires.

 Formal writing

 Write a step-by-step guide for building a pyramid

Looking at pyramid pictures

Teacher's intentions

● To learn about paintings inside pyramids;
● To discover what farmers did in Ancient Egypt.

Small group freeze frames: pyramid paintings

Explain to the children that they can now find out something about the workforce and that we know about the way the people farmed because of the paintings inside the pyramids. In small groups, children are given copies of pyramid drawings depicting farm labourers at work (see Figures 5.2, 5.3). The groups must first work out what the labourers are actually doing and then create the picture themselves by taking the positions of the figures in the pictures.

Figure 5.2 Pyramid drawings. N. de Garis Davies, *Ancient Egyptian Paintings*. Reproduced by permission of the Syndics of Cambridge University Library.

Figure 5.3 Pyramid drawings. N. de Garis Davies, *Ancient Egyptian Paintings*. Reproduced by permission of the Syndics of Cambridge University Library.

Once they have finished, arrange the children in rows on four sides so that they seem to be the pictures on the walls of the pyramid.

Freeze frames and teacher in role: presenting the pictures to an audience

You may like to invite another class into the space as visitors to the ancient pyramid. You can take the role as guide to draw attention to the different activities depicted in the pictures. The visitors may like to invite the magic of the place by going up to figures and asking them about what they are doing. It is best to keep these one at a time.

 Selecting details to answer questions

Write an explanation of the drawings for the pyramid museum to display beside the drawings

Embalming the Pharaoh and ending the story

Teacher's intentions

- To learn about Egyptian embalming;
- To recap on the information gathered about Ancient Egypt and the building of a pyramid.

This activity can be done with the whole class, with the teacher as the embalming priest if the children are younger or less mature, or alternatively in groups as described below.

Invite the children to imagine that time has passed, the pyramid is just completed and the Pharaoh has died. Children are divided into groups, given the embalming details (see below) and asked to enact the process. One child in each group pretends to be the priest who was in charge of the embalming process. As they work, the priest is teaching new embalmers how to do the job properly. They can use their bags, coats or one of themselves as the Pharaoh being embalmed. The group must ensure that all the processes are included, and that all the information provided on embalming is given to the new embalmers. They can make their scene as serious or comical as they like. The new embalmers can be good learners or bad!

The making of a mummy took seventy days, so the priest in the scene may say to his learners something like, 'Well, we will start today and, as I am sure you have been told, we will be doing this job for seventy days.'

Each of the three stages could be given to a different group and then performed in order.

Stage one
- The priest often wears a jackal mask during the embalming process. The jackal headed god is the god of mummification.
- Make a cut in the left side of the body to remove the organs that are likely to go bad, such as the stomach and lungs.
- A hook like a crochet hook is poked up the nostrils to remove the brain.

- The organs are to be placed into canopic jars. These are made of stone with lids depicting different gods, each protecting a different organ.

Stage two
- Natron, a preserving salt collected from the desert lakes, is put inside the body.
- Stitch up the body.
- Clean the body.
- Rub sweet-smelling liquid into the skin of the body to help preserve it.

Stage three
- Wrap the body in linen bandages. The quality and amount of linen used depends on the wealth and status of the dead person. A pharaoh will obviously have the most.
- Amulets must be wrapped between the layers of linen. A special one must be placed over the heart, such as an amulet depicting the scarab beetle often found in tomb paintings.
- The mummy is placed in its case. The dead person's portrait is painted on the case so that when his 'ka' spirit returns it will recognize its own body.

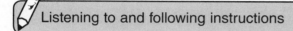
Listening to and following instructions

Look up the stages of the mummification process. Draw diagrams with notes to explain the process

Find out the meanings of some of the objects painted on to the case

Reflection: what have we learned?

Storytelling: using our knowledge to retell the story
As a whole class or in small groups, children tell the story of the details of the pyramid, the workforce and the process of embalming. You may conclude that once the embalmed body was placed in its chamber, all access points to the pyramid were completely sealed. Those who had completed the sealed doorways were, inevitably, killed to ensure that no living person knew where they were.

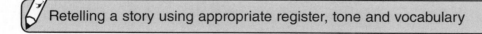
Retelling a story using appropriate register, tone and vocabulary

Small groups find out about one particular pyramid and prepare a presentation of information to the others. In this way children will hear about several constructions, such as the step pyramid made for King Djoser in about 2650 BC, and the Great Pyramid of King Khufu, which is big enough to enclose the main cathedrals of Milan, Rome, Florence and London.

Chapter 6
Life Cycles

Helena has never lived in the country before. Her flat in the city was great for views, but no good for learning about gardens and nature. When Helena moves into a tiny home in the country she is upset by the changes that occur in her garden. She doesn't know where the butterflies have gone, or why there are only flowers on the apple trees and no apples. The children are invited to help Helena understand the life cycles and teach her how to take care of her garden.

Learning objectives

- To learn to take into account the needs of listeners;
- To use explanatory language;
- To rehearse ordering and clarifying;
- To extend ideas in the light of discussion;
- To explore asking appropriate and relevant questions;
- To adapt speech for a specific audience.

Themes

- Life cycles
- Living things
- Plants and growth
- Environmental concerns.

Resources

- None.

Time

- This drama can be completed in one to one and a half hours.

Notes

The teacher playing Helena should appear perplexed and lacking in basic knowledge. At the same time, Helena is determined to understand and therefore asks searching questions. For example: 'But how can it be a chrysalis at one moment and then a butterfly the next?' She can appear to understand almost nothing and therefore she requires the children to explain the very basics first. It may be that the children need to do some research or drawings to clarify the processes they are trying to explain.

Introducing Helena and creating her garden

Teacher's intentions

- To set the scene of Helena and her garden;
- To create a garden through body and sound collage.

Narration: introducing Helena

Helena had lived in a busy city all her life. Her flat was at the very top of a high-rise block of flats. She was ready to retire and dreamed of having a really beautiful garden. Although she had enjoyed the views from the flat, she was sad never to have had a garden and wanted something really special. She only wanted a very small house, but, oh, how she dreamed of a lovely garden. It took a while taking train trips in different directions, but at last she found it: a tiny house with a perfect garden.

- *What do we understand about Helena?*
- *Where did she used to live?*
- *What did she want very very much?*
- *Where does she live now?*

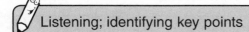 Listening; identifying key points

Defining space, dramatic construction and sound collage: creating the garden

Ask the children what the perfect garden might be like. What might be in it – a pond, lilies, roses, rabbits? Teacher continues questioning:

- *What sort of flowers?*
- *Are they scented?*
- *Whereabouts in the garden do they grow?*

Through this discussion the children generate an idea of the garden. From here, they create it, agreeing first where significant features are.

- *Is the pond in the middle?*
- *What did we say was growing near the pond?*
- *Where will the rose bush be?*

In pairs or small groups, the children need to:

- Decide what they will represent in the garden, such as the apple tree, the pond, the buttercups.
- Discuss words to describe what they are representing. A three-word minimum is a helpful limitation. Examples are: old, gnarled apple tree; scrambling, reaching, climbing roses.
- Become the feature. This could be still if they are representing a rockery or it could involve minimal movement. We have seen two children create a lily that opened by the children leaning and waving their arms back.
- Consider whereabouts they should be in the space, given the landmarks agreed earlier.
- Practise saying the words while in their positions.

Once the garden is created, explain that you will take the role of Helena walking around her garden. When she walks by, or stands by a pair/group, they should whisper their words. As she moves nearer the words get a bit louder, and as she moves away they get quieter and then fade away.

Teacher mimes opening a back door and walking outside, delighted, into the garden. She moves between the groups, perhaps dropping her hand into the pond and smelling the flowers. The words are whispered as she moves around the space, back and forth revisiting the different garden features. This creates a wonderful collage of sound as well as the physical picture. Finally, after a long happy look, Helena returns to her house.

Select words considering their sound and rhythm

Speak words considering tone and volume

The teacher and class create a large drawing of the garden, labelling its features

Pairs/groups plan a garden to scale on squared paper

Formal presentations of garden designs

Things seem to go wrong for Helena

Teacher's intentions

- To find out why Helena is so sad;
- To explore aspects of the life cycle.

Narration: introducing Helena's problem

That summer was very happy for Helena. She spent much of her time in the garden. Autumn arrived, then winter and into spring, but during this time, things had changed.

The neighbours hardly saw Helena. She spent no time in her garden at all. They couldn't understand it. Helena just stayed in her house. They began to peer through the window to see if she was all right. She was just sitting in her tiny room. She looked so sad. Some even thought they saw her crying. It was so strange, such a change from the Helena of before. Though the neighbours were worried, none of them had yet gone in.

Check the children's understanding of the narrative.

- *Where was Helena?*
- *Can we show what her expression might be?*
- *What might be wrong with her?*

Teacher in role and hot seating: finding out what's wrong with Helena

Tell the children that the neighbours decide to go to see Helena to try to find out what is wrong. The children will take the roles of the neighbours. Some discussion about what to say and how to approach Helena would be helpful.

- *What should we say first?*
- *What sort of mood do you think we should present?*
- *How will she know that we mean well?*
- *What sort of voices should we use, since she is upset?*

Explain that once you are sitting on a chair, you will be Helena and the drama can begin with one of the children knocking at an imaginary door. One child can be chosen to do this.

Helena is reluctant to speak to them. She is sure they don't want to come in. She is not in the mood for visitors. Once they are in, she only gradually responds to questions and explains that she is disappointed. She loved the garden, but it's all changed. She doesn't know much about gardens, but even she can see that it is not how it was. She presents particular anxieties. The children will deal with each one as it comes up. She may ask them many questions to help understand their explanations. Each time they will think that Helena should be happy and then she introduces another anxiety that they need to help her understand. The reasons for Helena's sadness are outlined below. The order in which they are discussed is not important.

Problem one: apple blossom → fruit
Last September there were lots of apples on the trees. It was wonderful. She used to pick one every day. But now there aren't any at all! The apple trees have got flowers on which are quite pretty, but where are the apples? She thought that the tree had died around Christmas because it went completely bare.

Problem two: frogspawn → tadpoles → frogs
She used to love watching the frogs around the pond, but now they are nowhere to be seen. In fact, the pond looks pretty revolting because it is full of slimy, jelly–mouldy stuff covered in nasty black spots. Helena can't believe the children's explanation that this will become frogs. It hasn't even got legs! And concerning tadpoles, she thinks they need their heads examined – frogs don't have tails!

Problem three: caterpillars → chrysalis → butterflies

Helena misses the butterflies. They used to look so pretty. Why have they left the garden? What has she done wrong? She used to sit beside the hedge and watch them fly around the sunflowers. Now she wouldn't even sit by the hedge because it is covered with squidgy green hairy things that walk in a strange loopy way.

Problem four: eggs → baby birds

You may have had enough after three problems, but this one always gives the children a smile. Helena is embarrassed that the children must think her a bit foolish for not understanding these things. However, she does know about eggs. As soon as she saw them in the nest she knew exactly what to do with them, but they have been in the fridge for two weeks and they still haven't hatched!

Asking appropriate and relevant questions

Explanation of processes

Children create charts to show the life cycle of frogs, fruit or butterflies. Pairs could cover different life forms

Read poems from *A Child's Garden of Verses* by Robert Louis Stevenson. Why is it called a garden of verses? Prepare shared readings

Clearing and recreating the garden

Teacher's intentions

- To engage the children in collective activity to put things right;
- To endorse learning about life cycles.

Teacher in role and whole group improvisation: working in the garden

Helena thanks the children for their advice and asks them if there are things she should be doing to care for her garden.

- *Should I move the leaves or will they keep the grass and flower beds warm?*
- *Does it matter that there are odd things growing between my rose beds?*
- *What can I do about the privet hedge being so tall and jagged on top that it looks ugly?*

The children offer or are asked to help with the garden. They all choose which jobs they will do, such as weeding, hedge cutting, raking the leaves and so on. Helena should move between them asking about what they are doing, offering help and telling them what a difference they are making. Finally, Helena thanks them for their help.

Freeze frame: recreating the garden

To round off this drama, the children can recreate the garden as they did earlier, using themselves to represent different features.

When they are still and in position, Helena walks around the garden saying how pleased she is that she has learned so much about her garden and about how things grow. She could give some detail of what she has learnt if the children need some points reinforced or clarified. If they were shaky on how a chrysalis is made, for example, she can explain it to herself aloud, perhaps as though she is looking at one. In this way, more information can be given.

> Speaking in role using appropriate register

> Research other life cycles, such as kangaroos, ducks
>
> Research and prepare a list of health and safety tips for working in the garden

Reflection: what have we learned?

Discuss what Helena's problems were and how the children helped her to solve them. Discuss the importance of having knowledge and understanding about the world.

Chapter 7
Reds and Greens

The children are in role as members of the Red community, hardworking and living in a happy and peaceful land: that is, until their ruler dies and is replaced by a Green leader, who decrees that things will have to change. The Reds will not be allowed to live and behave as before but will follow new Green laws, which go against their traditional practices. There is disruption in the community, unsettling their peaceful existence. The Reds have been put in a very difficult position. How will they respond?

Learning objectives

- To explore why and how laws are made and enforced;
- To recognize the consequences of antisocial and aggressive behaviour, such as bullying and racism, on individuals and communities;
- To reflect on moral, social and cultural issues, using imagination to understand other people's experiences.

Themes

- Democracy
- Power.

Resources

- Red stickers;
- Green stickers;
- Red cloak, scarf, jumper or other item;
- Green cloak, scarf, jumper or other item;
- A large book with a red cover;
- A scroll with the decree written on it (see Figure 7.1).

Time

- The whole session takes about one and a half hours.

Notes

This drama raises a number of difficult issues to do with prejudice, imposing ideas on others, loyalty and freedom to follow your own beliefs. Issues concerned with repression, ethnic cleansing, religious, racial and political freedom can be raised through this session, depending on your focus.

Originally, this drama was written as a way into the religious issues raised during the Tudor and Stuart period in British history, which resulted in the Gunpowder Plot. It is useful to bear this in mind, though, since the struggle between the Reds and the Greens closely echoes that between the Catholics and the Protestants. However, it has far wider possible connections.

The colours red and green have been chosen as clearly different and identifiable colours but any two contrasting colours, shapes or symbols can be chosen if these two are not appropriate for your situation. The Suns and the Moons, the Circles and the Triangles, the Purples and the Yellows are all perfectly acceptable. Suitable stickers and cloaks (or other token items of costume) will need to be found.

Setting the scene – the people of the Red land

Teacher's intentions

● To introduce the idea of belonging and identity.

Ritual and teacher in role: setting the scene

The children stand in a circle and, one at a time, are solemnly and formally given red stickers to wear. Tell them that in the drama these are known as emblems and are worn with great pride.

Tell the children that they are all people of the Red land waiting on the quiet hillside outside their village for an important event to occur. Tell them that you will walk away and then return to the circle in role as someone that they all know, and you will speak to them. They must listen carefully to pick up clues and information to find out more about the drama and who they are in it.

Walk away from the circle, put on the red cloak and slowly return, smiling calmly, looking positive and authoritative. Address the people:

My friends, people of the Red land. We gather here today on this quiet hillside as we do every year to think about our precious Red land and the Queen who rules so fairly and justly over us all. We think of what it means to be a Red and how important our Red laws have become, helping to keep our community safe and happy for so long. These Red laws that we all live by were written down in the time of Aelfric the Red, our first leader, and agreed on by all of the people. The law decrees that we should wear our Red emblems with pride, eat the food of the Reds, wear the clothes of the Reds and lead our lives in the ways agreed.

 Listen and identify key points

Write a list of key points

Discussion: what have we learned?

Take off the cloak and sit down in a circle. Ask the group about what has just happened. They could talk first with partners before sharing.

- *Who are the people standing on the hillside?*
- *Why are the people wearing red emblems?*
- *Who was the person in the red cloak?*
- *What event is taking place?*
- *Is there any sense of a time period for the drama?*
- *What gives this impression?*
- *What could the speaker have meant about the Red laws? What could they be?*
- *Why could it be that these laws are so important to the Reds?*
- *What sort of community is this?*

Issues concerning why and how rules and laws are made can be discussed here.

> Recall and represent important points

> Write down key points as a record
>
> Note key vocabulary, e.g. loyalty. Use a thesaurus and dictionary.

Freeze frames with captions: the Red laws

Tell the class that you are going to discover more about the Red land and its people, in particular their laws. Discuss possibilities such as:

- eating Red food;
- wearing Red clothes;
- rituals to remember the great Aelfric the Red;
- a Red celebration;
- a Red greeting.

Divide the class into small groups of four or five. Ask each group to decide on one aspect of the Red law and create a freeze frame to show the other groups. You could tell the children that these pictures are taken from a book about the Red land and its people and that it illustrates aspects of their culture. If you have a large red book, use this as a prop. Ask each group to think of the caption that would go underneath their picture.

Each group shows their picture and the rest of the class tries to decide upon what is being shown. The captions are then read. Teacher introduces each new picture solemnly and thanks each group for showing an important aspect of the Red law.

After all of the pictures have been viewed, reiterate the importance of the laws and how important the book of Red Law is to the people.

> Use dramatic techniques to explore characters and feelings

Captions can be written on a large piece of paper

Write a legend about Aelfric the Red, which tells of his strength and wisdom

The Red laws and customs can be written in a list

A threat to the peace of the Red land

Teacher's intentions

● To present a challenge to the group.

Teacher in role and meeting

Ask the group to reform the circle and tell them that in the next part of the drama you will be someone that they haven't met before. Leave the circle and put on the Green cloak. Return to the circle carrying the scroll. Try to create a different atmosphere this time. Walk slowly and look around at the Reds as though they were beneath you. Be powerful and aloof, perhaps threatening, but not over the top! Slowly unroll the scroll and read.

> The Queen of this land is dead. The new King decrees that from this day no one is to wear the clothes of the Reds, eat the food of the Reds or follow any of the Red laws as written by Aelfric the Red, the first leader of the Red people. The people of the Red land must never again wear their Red emblems or gather together on the quiet hillside as they have done in the past each year. They will now abide by the laws of the Green King and wear Green emblems or risk severe punishment. The Reds have been warned!
>
> King James

Figure 7.1 The Green message

Tell the Reds that you are able to answer a few questions before you leave, but as you are only the messenger you have no real answers. Any difficult questions that are asked can be answered with a cutting phrase such as:

● *You have been told what will happen if you do not obey.*
● *There is no option.*
● *You have no choice.*
● *The King has decreed so that is the end to it.*

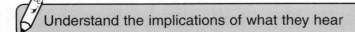

Understand the implications of what they hear

Thought tunnel: how do we feel about this?

Ask the group to stand in two parallel lines facing each other with enough space for you to walk down the 'path' that has been created. Explain that you are going to walk down this path as though you were the Green messenger leaving the village. Ask them to speak their thoughts about the situation such as:

- *This is terrible.*
- *They can't do this.*
- *I'm not going to follow any Green laws.*
- *I'll always be a Red.*

As the Green messenger passes along the path he puts a Green sticker or emblem on to each Red and announces: *You will follow the laws of the Green King and wear the Green emblem.*

 Speaking in role, communication of feelings and emotions

Record responses in speech bubbles

Discussion: what has happened so far?

Out of role, discuss what could be done.

- *How would the Reds be feeling?*
- *What could they really do about the situation?*
- *What would it feel like to be told you couldn't be yourself any more?*

(We have found that the children usually say they would fight against the Greens, and the effectiveness of this approach should be discussed. The King is Green and the power is therefore in Green hands.)

 Shape and organize an argument

Record responses and evaluate or them

Look up useful words – rebel, dissident, etc.

Compose a letter from the Red people to the Green king to plead their case

The Reds talk in secret

Teacher's intentions

- To deepen discussion and responses.

Overheard conversations: listening to the thought of the Reds

Ask the children to sit in small groups and discuss the feelings of the Reds, in role. Ask them to think what the Reds would try to do about the situation. Tell them that you will walk around the village in role as the Green messenger, so they must be careful about what they say when you are near. Give all of the groups a few minutes to practise their improvised conversations. Ask each group in turn to talk while the rest listen. As you walk up to the group the subject of the conversation should change quickly to avoid you hearing any Red dissident talk.

 Careful listening, concentrating on volume and tone

Rumour-mill: spreading rumours around the Red village

Ask the groups to repeat their conversations and this time you will change your cloak and once again be a Red. Go from group to group joining in the conversations and stirring up dissatisfaction.

I'm not going to sit back and take orders from the Green king. Meet me tonight on the quiet hillside to discuss a plan.

 Expressing opinions

Recording feelings in thought or speech bubbles

Narration, teacher in role and meeting: challenging the Green king

Teacher narrates:

That night, under the cover of darkness, every single member of the Red people gathered together to discuss what they could do.

Teacher in role as the Red subversive welcomes the Reds and collects them all together, encouraging quietness and secrecy by whispering, looking around nervously, and possibly crouching down.

Develop your subversive role, stirring up anti-Green feeling. Encourage them to wear their Red emblems and throw away the Green ones.

Remember Aelfric and the Red laws. What would he say to see you all forgetting so quickly?

We have found that some children are quick to join the subversives while others are more wary, being mindful of the warning that the Green messenger made and wanting a quiet life. This debate can go on for as long as it is productive and exploring new ideas or possibilities.

Teacher in role: the Reds are caught out

Quickly, ask the children to re-form the circle as in the first activity. Change your cloak to Green and rapidly re-enter the circle. Look searchingly around the circle and pick out those who are wearing the Red emblems. Make them stand at one side of the room.

Announce to those who are wearing Red emblems:

You were warned. Now you will be punished!

Appropriate responses

Write a diary entry recording the events of the day

What will the future hold?

Teacher's intension

● To represent features of an argument in a symbolic way.

Discussion and circle of thoughts: hearing the thoughts of the Reds

Lead a discussion about what has happened. This could be done in pairs to begin with.

● *What do the children think will happen to the Red dissidents?*
● *What will the rest feel?*
● *How will life change for the Reds?*

Tell the children that to finish off the drama they are going to speak the thoughts and feelings of the Red people. Place a chair in the middle of the room with the red book on it. Ask the children to stand either in a circle around the chair or randomly around the room. If you choose to ask them to stand randomly, ask them to think about how near to the book they want to stand. This will be determined by how loyal they feel towards Aelfric or how much they feel they have betrayed or distanced themselves from the Red laws. Some may also choose to stand with their backs to the book or some may want to kneel down.

When the positions have been chosen, you will go around and touch each child on the shoulder. The children will speak aloud the thoughts of their roles.

● *I know I have betrayed Aelfric's laws.*
● *I feel dreadful.*
● *What could we have done? I'll always wear a Red emblem under my cloak.*
● *I feel alright in my new Green life.*

Reflection: what have we learned?

It is important to spend some time after the drama has finished discussing the issues raised and relating this story to a historical or topical context.

Expressing opinions

Write an account of life under Green rule

Additional drama activity

Imagine that an old Green book is discovered. It contains pictures and captions, just like the Red book. In groups, children make the Green pictures as they did for the Red book. Green laws can be written.

Chapter 8
Charles I

Charles I is the only British monarch ever to have been charged with treason and to have been beheaded. He dismissed his parliament in 1635 to ensure he could do things his own way. This meant no legal processes for charging taxes without parliament, so he further made himself unpopular by raising money illegally. He prosecuted his opponents, made enemies within the Church of England with his intolerance of those who were not as High Church (leaning towards Roman Catholicism) as he, and finally, he alienated the Army. Parliament had had enough – he was found guilty of treason and was beheaded on January 30 1649.

This drama is not about the King's life, but about the few words he spoke at the trial. Historians have the evidence of these words, but when the children consider them and enact them, we find that historical evidence of the spoken word provides only half of the story. How were the words spoken, and what did the King's body language communicate? Does this 'evidence' mean very much?

Learning objectives

- To understand that text can be spoken in different ways to communicate different things;
- To explore how body language, gesture and eye contact impact on communication;
- To have the opportunity to deliver text of historical value.

Themes

- Communication
- Historical enquiry.

Resources

- Copies of the text provided on sheets for each child and perhaps on a screen, too;
- Highlighter pens.

Time

- One hour.

The King is charged with treason

Teacher's intentions

- To explain the context for the work.

Narration: the scene is set

Provide the information that is held early in the paragraphs above as narration. You may wish to introduce further information from your own knowledge or research, too.

Our scene is set in parliament in 1649. Those in parliament were doing what had never been done before. They were charging their King, Charles I, with treason. One way and another, the King had upset many people, and this included many people who had the power to do something. Parliament took a risk, since this had never happened before ... But they brought him in for trial and asked him questions. He said very little, declining to ask their questions. We do have, however, some of the words that historians know he said that day. He talked about the right of Kings as something given by God, which he saw gave him rights above others to rule.

Discuss the information given so far:

- *What does treason mean?*
- *What might life have been like in 1649? Were there cars? What did people wear?*
- *What might the King have chosen to say since he said so very little? [Suggestions may include: 'I'm innocent.' 'Who do you think you are?' 'I am your King.']*

Let's explore this moment in time through drama.

> Look for pictures of Charles I on the internet

The King's response

Teacher's intentions

- To introduce the words of Charles I;
- To enable children to overcome anxiety about the unfamiliarity of the words;
- Develop concentration and swift responses.

> *I wish to know by what power I am brought here – I would know what lawful authority. Remember I am your king, your lawful king ... I say think well upon it ... I have a trust committed to me by God, by old and lawful descent. I will not betray it to a new and unlawful authority.*

Figure 8.1

Collaborative reading and conducting: what the King said

Give out the copies of the text in Figure 8.1 or present it on a screen where all the children can see it. Ask them all to read it aloud together, not worrying about meaning at this stage. Read it through aloud altogether a few times. It is important that you do not read the text aloud on your own because this would provide an interpretation of it, which is being left open for the class to consider.

Using a baton, a paintbrush or a stick, explain that you will be like a conductor. But instead of conducting a musical orchestra, you will conduct them reading the text. You will gesture with your baton when they are to start saying the words, and when they are to stop. You can thus stop the speech at random moments and leave pauses as you chose. When they reach the end, they simply read from the beginning again.

When the children have gained confidence in this, introduce volume. You will indicate when they are to change the volume. For examples, raise your hands up when you wish them to read more loudly, and lower them if you wish the children to be quieter. They have to concentrate hard to ensure they are responding and keeping in with the others with volumes and pauses. Children love to take a turn to be the conductor and enjoy the sense of holding the whole class in their power with the baton!

By this time, the children will have become fairly familiar with the words without having realised it or consciously tried to understand them. The lines are now not daunting, since they are no longer unfamiliar.

> Reading aloud with emphasis on volume, pace and pauses

> Use a dictionary to look up any unknown words

Discussion: what might the King have been feeling?

The King would never have imagined that he would have been charged by parliament, and would never have dreamt that he might be at risk of a beheading! This is what would happen if he was found guilty.

While he was saying these lines, what might he have been feeling?

- *Scared?*
- *Angry?*
- *Outraged?*
- *Incensed?*

The children discuss these and may refer to some of the words still displayed.

> Deduction, interpreting, vocabulary extension

> Using a thesaurus, generate a list of synonyms – annoyed, irritable, snappy bad-tempered, irritated, petulant

Group work: choosing the feeling behind the lines

Paper copies of the text are required. In groups of three or four, the children choose what mood the King could have been in, using the ideas from the discussion. They should not let other groups know their decisions.

They then highlight or underline the words they think should be emphasized to give the feeling they have chosen. They discuss the following:

● *Which words for emphasis?*
● *Where should there be pauses?*
● *Where should there be louder and softer speaking?*
● *Where should there be faster or slower speaking?*

Each group prepares a group reading that emphasizes the feeling they selected. They will then read it to the other groups, facing away, so that no signs beyond the aural are communicated. The audience could close their eyes as they listen to each other's work. Each group may choose to guess what feeling the King has in each reading.

 Reading aloud with focus on register, tone and emphasis

Playing the scene

Teacher's intentions

● To invite consideration of how gesture communicates;
● To consider how audience and space affects communication.

Preparing the role: How did King Charles deliver his words?

Consider the many ways that gestures and body language could affect the meaning of the words.

● *How is his head held?*
● *What does he do with his hands? Are they threatening or challenging?*
● *Or do they show regret, dangling limply beside him? Are they clenched or pointing?*
● *Does he move while he speaks?*
● *Does he move towards or away from the crowds judging him?*

In the same groups, children prepare one group member to be King Charles I. He or she will be directed to deliver the lines as planned in the previous activity, but now with actions. Do not perform these until after the next activity.

Preparing the role: how did King Charles arrive in the parliament?

King Charles entered the parliament, where there were people on three sides. Invite the children to consider the ways that he might have entered the space:

- *Did he look up or down?*
- *Did he make eye contact with the Parliamentarians?*
- *Did he avoid eye contact?*
- *Did he stand hunched or tall?*
- *Did he walk strongly or weakly, with heavy or light steps?*
- *Were his movements fast or slow?*

While discussing these, there may be some discussion about what the different possibilities might say about the King and his mood and attitude.

The groups now work together to consider how their King will enter parliament.

 Using body language to convey different meanings

Look at photographs from newspapers and magazines and suggest how people are feeling from their body language

Performing the role: what impression might King Charles have given?

Arrange the space with chairs on three sides, leaving a space for the King to enter. The group performers take it in turns to enter and deliver their lines.

Usually, you will find considerable differences between each performance. There will be much to talk about.

- *Did you feel more sympathy for some? More dislike for others?*
- *Were the same words selected for emphasis?*
- *How did they use the space and what did that tell you about the King?*
- *What did the performers do to appear more confident? Defiant?*

 Focus on body language and facial expression to convey meaning

Discuss the importance of facial expression and body language in communication

Research Charles I

Write a reply to Charles's words, as written by the parliamentarians

Reflection: What have we learned?

- *How much does the historical evidence tell us about this extraordinary moment in history?*
- *What have we learned about the use of words?*
- *Can you think of examples of things we say to each other that mean different things with different gestures? 'I like you' can be said sarcastically, kindly, deceitfully, for example. Experiment with different ways of delivering these words. 'I'm sorry' is another good one to experiment with.*

Chapter 9
World War II: The Home Front

Life in Britain is very different with the war on. Mrs Violet Lynch, afraid for the safety of her husband who is away fighting in France, is bewildered by a present she receives from him. A young friend, Rosie, is struggling to follow the requirements of living in a time of rationing. She tries to save her bread ration, but gets in trouble with the authorities, who are checking that pig swill bins are used appropriately. These incidents are based on real people's lives in the Midlands, England.

Learning objectives

- To explore some of the social implications of World War II;
- To consider the impact of food rationing;
- To develop empathy.

Themes

- The Home Front
- Food
- Loss.

Resources

- Envelope addressed to Mrs Lynch, 22 Victoria Road, Northampton. It contains a photocopy of the telegram provided (Figure 9.2);
- Brown cloth;
- Copy of note on an envelope provided to Vi from Ned;
- Chair and table for mimed scene.

Time

- One and a half hours.

Notes

Be sure to read the statement by Maureen Micklethwaite below before starting. The drama is based on her story. You may wish to use selected activities, say the Mrs Lynch story, or just the rationing story. They can be taught independently of others. You will also need to be familiar with the actions required by civilians before taking the role of Mr Farnsbarn. Details are provided below, but there is plenty more on the internet!

Mrs Lynch receives a telegram

Teacher's intentions

- To build belief in a person in a historical context;
- To introduce the idea of loss during war time;
- To introduce the central character of the drama.

Maureen Micklethwaite wrote in 1992:

> *The story as told to me by my mother.*
>
> *We lived in London – my father worked for the Gas Company and was a rifleman in the Territorial Army in a company/battalion that was attached to the Gasworks.*
>
> *When the war began these territorials were among the first to be enlisted. Before the war they enjoyed a good life. My father would take part in shooting competitions and he spent the evenings with my mother playing the piano and everyone joining in a sing-song: 'You are my heart's delight' and 'Only a shanty in an old shanty town', and many more. There was plenty to eat and sherry for the ladies and beer for the men. Our home was a popular venue.*
>
> *In 1940 France capitulated and my father was not happy leaving the family in London, so we came to Northamptonshire to be with him as his regiment prepared to embark abroad. On November 11th 1940, the regiment left Northampton – my mother did not know where they were going. Just as my father was leaving, my parents received the news that our home in London had been bombed. My father's last words to my mother were to remain in Northampton until he came back.*
>
> *My mother wrote to my father regularly but he never received any of her letters. In fact, they were all returned to her much later. The only news she had was a telegram (see below). One day she received a parcel supposedly from my father. When she opened it, she saw a brown table cover. She says the cloth was an omen of bad luck. She feels sure that my father would not have chosen that colour since he knew how superstitious she was and never bought anything in brown. Even when she received the news that my father was missing, she hung on to the hope that he might be a prisoner of war.*
>
> *Most of the company of men with my father in Greece in 1941 were wiped out through lack of air cover.*
>
> *My mother has remained in Northampton. As she says, 'Your father told me to stay here.'*

Mimed action: introducing Mrs Lynch

Teacher takes role of Mrs Lynch, sitting in a chair. The addressed envelope is placed on the floor some distance away from the chair, as though it is on the door mat. Beside the chair, on a table is the note from Ned (see Figure 9.1 below) and the brown cloth.

Ask the children to watch in silence and to try to work out what might be happening. The mime is as follows:

Mrs Lynch sits on the chair pensively. She looks at the note from Ned, then looks away again, then holds the note close to her, looking very upset. After a while, her eye catches the envelope and she hurries forward, but seeing the typed address she slows down. Slowly, she picks up the letter and returns to the chair looking at and fingering the envelope seemingly wondering whether or not to open it. She turns to the brown cloth, takes it on to her lap folding and unfolding it, still looking at the envelope. At last she hugs the envelope and brown cloth and rocks forward and back on the chair. She is perhaps weeping.

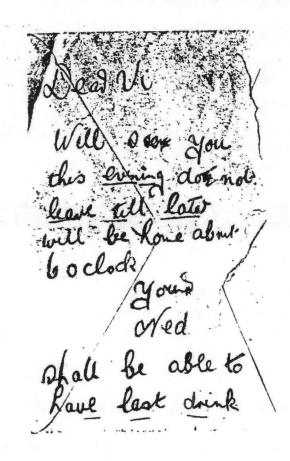

Figure 9.1

Hot seating: what is Mrs Lynch thinking about?

Out of role, ask the children what they saw and how they thought Mrs Lynch was feeling. Ask follow-up questions as they give their ideas to clarify ideas for everyone.

Invite children to speak to Mrs Lynch. What might they ask and say to her? How should they speak given how upset she is?

As Mrs Lynch, sit on the chair and respond to pupils' questions. Tell them about her life from the story provided above. She can read them the last note that Ned wrote to her on an envelope. Holding it makes her feel close to him. The reason that she hasn't opened the letter may be that she is afraid of what it might contain. She doesn't dare open it. Her friend will be coming soon because they both have to attend a meeting at the town hall about the precautions that must be taken during the time of war. Her friend, Rosie, also thinks that she may get some ideas of what to do with the powdered egg they are being given with their ration books. She will delay opening the letter until she gets back from the meeting. She cannot bear to look at the envelope.

The hot seating ends when questions have been asked and the information has been communicated.

Leave Mrs Lynch's chair and re-enter the space out of role for a discussion of what the children have found out and what they feel they still do not understand.

Prediction

Using appropriate language in difficult context

Listen to understand what is not said as well as what is

Write what might be in the envelope

List what we know and what we do not know

Update the lists of what we know and do not know. Ideas could be recorded using a Role on the Wall

Civilians' responsibilities for the war effort

Teacher's intentions

- To inform the children of food rationing;
- To provide the context of the Home Front;
- To engage children in consideration of how civilians' lives changed as they played their part.

Meeting in role: what are you doing for the war effort?

The room is arranged for the meeting in the Town Hall. Explain that you will take on a new role as a town council official, Mr Farnsbarn. The official has to provide details about how civilians should behave, about food supplied to civilians and rations.

Mr Farnsbarn is officious. The teacher should get over as much information as is appropriate to the class. Details are provided below. Pupils in role as adults should be encouraged to comment and question throughout the meeting. They could answer direct questions:

- What do you use to blackout your windows?
- You've got tomatoes in your window boxes, haven't you?
- What do you put into the pigbins?

Open the meeting in the following way:

You all have responsibilities as serious as those who are away fighting. You have responsibilities to behave in all ways to support our soldiers and the nation's interests. Just because you are still on British soil does not mean that you do not have work to do.

Then relay the following information or selections of it depending on the age and ability of the children:

Food is limited because:

- *Ships were sunk during the war [less foreign foods were arriving into UK ports];*
- *Cattle were slaughtered [as they are an inefficient use of land];*
- *Tractors and fertilizers were rationed as resources were limited.*

Intersperse information with questions about what you have explained to the townspeople.

- Do they understand the implications of this?
- If cattle are slaughtered, which meats will not be available during the war?
  Well, listen to me ...
  The following foods that are scarce: oranges, meat, butter, sugar, cheese, eggs, chocolate. The following foods are available, though limited: dried egg, pork, horsemeat, vegetables, spam, fish from local waters, milk.
- Do they know what to do with dried egg?
- Have they eaten horsemeat before?
- Do they know how to make cakes without sugar?
- Have they any idea about which foods are scarce?
- Which foods have they been missing?

Explain what rationing means and offer the following advice for dealing with this difficult context:

- *Carrots must be used instead of sugar in cakes;*
- *Money given for old jars and rags as nothing must be wasted;*
- *'Kitchen Front' on the radio gives ideas for recipes*
- *Food can be grown in window boxes (tomatoes) and on bomb sites (marrows);*
- *Allotments – families are encouraged to dig for their country;*
- *Keep your own chickens on roofs, balconies, etc.*

Mr Farnsbarn turns particularly nasty:

No food should be placed in bins. All food waste MUST be placed in the 'pig bins' so that it supports the rearing of pigs. I am shocked to know that one lady here in this very hall failed to dispose of her waste food in the proper way. This is disgraceful and reveals a person who seems not to care about the war effort and our boys fighting to preserve our nation's freedom. She has been fined four shillings for throwing stale bread in a dustbin instead of the pig bin!

- What would you wish to say to such a woman?

No one must bribe the butchers. I am shocked to have learned that some women have been trying to get more than their rations by offering bribes to the butchers. This is unfair.
  You may wish to include some more general points, checking that the public understand why these are important:

- Blackouts;

- Car headlights to be covered except for slits;
- Anderson shelters, gas masks;
- 'Careless talk costs lives';
- 'Make do and mend'.

Advising, encouraging, suggesting

Listening for facts

Interpreting meaning

Make posters promoting behaviour to support the war effort

Look up recipes for food during the rationing

Create a recipe book with each child contributing a recipe

A woman is guilty

Teacher's intentions

- To consider the difficulties of great life changes;
- To consider the story behind a headline.

Statementing: what do we think about that woman?

Place a chair in the centre of the space and ask the children to stand in a circle around it. You could place a handbag or hat on the chair explaining that it represents the woman we all heard about who has the four-shilling fine. Check they recall what she was fined for. Then invite them to step towards the chair in turn and say what they think about her, or what they would say to her. Then they return to the circle.

How might the woman feel to know what people are saying about her?

Giving opinions, describing emotions

Hot seating: why did Rosie do such a thing?

Explain to the class that Mrs Lynch's friend, Rosie, is the woman who received a letter asking her to report to the Ministry of Food office to pay the four-shilling fine. Rosie was seen wiping her eyes many times during the meeting. She heard Mr Farnsbarn's comments and what others are saying and is very distressed. Could the children try to find out what happened from her side of the story?

Explain that you will take the role of Rosie and the children can ask you questions. As Rosie, do not necessarily trust them at first, and delay giving information until you feel they won't throw it back at you.

The context (based on a factual case) that you can gradually unfold is as follows:

I have only been married for a few months. There is a lot to learn to keep a home and I have tried very hard to do everything right. I am also trying to obey the new instructions about playing my part in the war effort. I want to do right. I am so horrified that people will know I wasted half a loaf. They will think I do not care.

In fact, I was responding to the problem of rationing. I had collected a loaf from the baker with my ration book. I knew to make it last as long as possible since there wouldn't be another very soon. Hence, I ensured we only ate a small amount at a time, and I kept the remainder in a tin. But I kept it too long. It went stale and black bits appeared on it. I was upset that I had wasted the limited bread ration. I couldn't drop it into the pig bin since people would see it and be angry that I had wasted the bread. I felt angry with myself anyway. So I wrapped it up and put it in the normal refuse bin and I thought no one would know. I didn't know authorities were checking the bins.

It wasn't that I took rationing lightly. Really, all this happened because I took it very seriously. But now I am in trouble. I feel ashamed.

You may conclude that even your friend Violet Lynch seemed distant from you today. She said very little, so she may not wish to be your friend anymore. The children may explain that Mrs Lynch has her own worries.

> Speaking and listening sensitively

> Write Rosie's diary of the day she found the bread was mouldy
>
> Sequencing by writing a list of the events that led to the fine

Mrs Lynch opens the letter

Teacher's intentions

- To conclude the story of Mrs Lynch's letter;
- To empathize with a character;
- To consider narrative and stream of consciousness.

Shared narration and stream of consciousness: approaching the letter

This is quite a complex dramatic activity, but very powerful. The pupils need to know what they have to do throughout, before they start, so it runs smoothly. The aim is for you to play Mrs Lynch in her room opening her letter and reacting to it, according to the class's directions. The children provide the narrative description of the scene and you respond to this (e.g. *She gets up from her chair*). An additional option is for the children to also provide the 'stream of consciousness' of her thoughts during the scene (e.g. *I can't delay opening it any longer*).

The children stand in a circle. Place the chair and table as before with the letter on the table. Mrs Lynch starts outside the circle. The pupils in turn narrate what Mrs Lynch is doing and the teacher responds accordingly.

For example, pupil 1: *She stood still staring at the letter.*

Pupil 2: *She put her hands over her face and sighed.*

The pupils need to understand that whilst they can narrate Mrs Lynch about to open the letter, then not doing so, they cannot have her actually opening it. With older children you can have the pupils alternating narration with Mrs Lynch's thoughts.

For example, pupil 1: *She stood still staring at the letter.*

Pupil 2: *It might not be bad news – perhaps he's coming home.*

Pupil 3: *She puts her hands over her face and sighs.*

Pupil 4: *Ned, Ned, please be coming home.*

After each pupil has spoken Mrs Lynch then tears the envelope open and takes the telegram and reads it out loud (Figure 9.2). There should be a few moments' silence before stopping the drama. Mrs Lynch may even weep.

Effects Form 100 B-2.

No. D/54636 (Effects)

CERTIFIED that having regard to such information as is available concerning No: 6002089, Regimental Sergeant-Major Edmund Lynch. King's Royal Rifle Corps.

who was officially reported missing on 28th April. 1941 ~~it has been~~

presumed by the War Office that he died was killed in action on between 26th & 28th April 1941

in at Sea. while serving with the British

Expeditionary Force.

A. Nicholson

Given at the WAR OFFICE

this 22nd day of August 1942

(19100) Wt.26073,2320 5,000 8/41 A.A.E.W.Ltd. Gp.693

Figure 9.2

Using different forms of language – narration (third person) and (first person) feelings

Construct descriptive sentences to describe Mrs Lynch immediately prior to opening the letter

Create a timeline for the wall providing the actions of Mrs Lynch with the feelings below and above. At the end, provide a copy of the telegram

Freeze frames/photographs: Mrs Lynch remembers happier times

Explain that after reading the letter, Mrs Lynch got out some photographs to remember happy times with her husband, Ned. Ask the children to work in groups to prepare a photograph that she may have, such as their child's birthday, her husband in uniform with his regiment, or a beach picnic, etc. Check you know what each group is portraying so you can create a chronological order. Let the groups know the order.

Take the role of Mrs Lynch on her chair, looking through an imaginary album of photographs. As you turn an imaginary page, a group will stand up and create their freeze frame. Provide an appropriate monologue to link the photos and place them in her context

Ah, yes. I was never happier than at our wedding day. Ned looks so serious/happy/ proud

whatever is appropriate to the freeze frame. When that page is turned the first group disappear and the next group take their place.

The monologue would be on the lines of, *Oh, our first holiday with the baby. It was cold* [laughs] *but we had such fun.* [Pause] *Life looked so promising then.* [Mimes turning the page] *The last time I saw him. To think I was excited to see him in uniform. Ned, please come back to us.*

Reflection: what have we learned?

There are many aspects of this drama to be considered in terms of what has been learned.

Regarding history, you may ask clarifying questions:

- What does the term civilian mean (civvies/civvie street)?
- What do you now understand by the term 'Home Front'?
- Why was the letter addressed to Mrs *Edward* Lynch, and not Mrs Violet Lynch, which was her name?
- Are there other things from the drama that seem to be different from the way we do things today?
- How was life different during the war for people like Mrs Lynch and Rosie?
- What is meant by food rationing? What was rationed?
- What other behaviours to you recall Mr Farnsbarn explaining?

Regarding empathy and relationships:

- What single words describe how Mrs Lynch felt when she read the letter?
- Do you feel that Mr Farnsbarn's attitude to Rosie fair? Why?
- What have we learned about simple accusations?
- What would you like to say to Rosie to make her feel better?

> Create a class newspaper for this day with articles about the fine and recipe ideas, etc.
>
> Research stories set in the UK during World War II
>
> Write stories set during this period in the Home Front

Chapter 10
Is Emma's Friend Stealing?

Emma is in a dilemma. Her best friend, Liz, seems to have a lot of new things, but how has she come by them? Emma has heard others at school talking about Liz and fear that perhaps she is stealing. She takes the difficult decision to speak to her and to her teacher, but Liz still goes into town and into a boutique in a department store and considers what to steal. We consider the implications of Liz's actions.

Learning objectives

- To consider implications of stealing;
- To try different language registers.

Themes

- Law and order
- Friendship
- Morality.

Resources

- Emma's diary entry: see example (see Figure 10.1).

Time

- Two hours.

Discovering a page from a diary

Teacher's intentions

- To consider what can be understood from the diary extract;
- To introduce Emma and her worries.

Diary and discussion

Explain that the children are going to do a drama that involves the writer of a diary.

- *What is a diary?*
- *Who writes diaries?*
- *Why do people keep diaries?*
- *Do any of you keep a diary or know anyone who does?*

Read the date and diary entry written by Emma, explaining that this is not a real person's diary, but a character in the drama.

November 12th

Dear Diary,

I feel really worried. I know Liz has been stealing. It's obvious. She's had a new pencil case. Felt pens and everything. She's making loads of new friends (that's what she thinks) 'cos she's always got loads of sweets. She can't have enough money to buy them all. After all the time we've been best friends and I feel that I can't say anything to her. I've wanted to say something but I just can't. Today was horrid 'cos I heard other people calling her a thief. They actually used that word. Oh, I just don't know what to say.

Got 7 out of 10 for my maths test today, but I couldn't feel pleased with all this Liz business going on.

Good night, Diary.

From a very worried Emma.

Figure 10.1

Ask the children what they know about Emma and Liz and how Emma feels. Teacher then asks them if they think Emma should say anything to Liz. Facilitate discussion on what she might say to avoid outright confrontation with her friend, and consider what she could say.

Interpreting written text

Considering diary as a genre

Look at examples of diaries, fictional diaries, such as Adrian Mole's by Sue Townsend; personal diaries used to calendarize; genuine diaries, such as an extract from a political diary of Richard Crossland, Tony Benn or Tony Blair.

Conversations at school

Teacher's intentions

- To consider tactful approaches in conversation;
- To experiment with finding the appropriate words.

Teacher in role

Re-iterate what the children have discussed as a good approach to open up the subject with Liz. Place two chairs, explaining that one represents Emma and the other is for Liz. You will take the role of Liz and the class share the voice of Emma. To jointly take on the voice of Emma, the class arrange themselves in a semi-circle behind Emma's chair, and any one of them can speak in any order, one at a time. Explain that it will be hard for you, as Liz, to respond if there is more than one voice at a time. You will talk as though to someone on the chair rather than look at the individuals who are speaking.

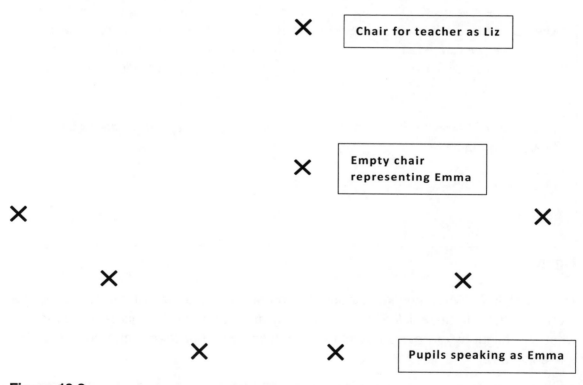

Figure 10.2

Let the class try different approaches to start the conversation with Emma.

- *Hello Liz. I want to speak to you.*
- *I'm glad we're alone because I want to speak to you.*
- *Please don't be angry.*

Liz should not make it easy for Emma. She could respond in a hostile, even aggressive way, accusing Emma of being a poor friend for even thinking such things. Eventually, Liz should storm out.

> Experimenting with language and tone of voice in sensitive situations
>
> Listening to interpret mood and implication behind what is said and how it is said and finding appropriate responses

> Write a script between the two friends using ideas from the practical work
>
> Read Jacqueline Wilson's *Secrets,* a novel about two unlikely friends

Paired improvisation: conversations between Emma and her teacher

Explain that during the afternoon lessons Emma was very upset. At the end of school Emma's teacher asked her what was the matter and why she wasn't sitting with Liz. What might Emma say? The class are then asked to work in pairs, A and B.

As take the role of Emma and Bs the teacher. Then each pair needs to find a space and have the conversation that might have taken place between the two.

After a while the class should return to one circle and discuss what happened. How many teachers found out the truth? How had they questioned Emma? Had the Emmas who told the truth felt they'd done right or did they feel some sense of disloyalty?

Liz goes to town

Teacher's intentions

- To explore the implications of attempting to steal;
- To engage children to contribute ideas to a class activity.

Defining space and whole class improvisation: in the shop

Teacher narrates:

Liz felt angry all afternoon. She kept away from Emma and didn't wait for her by the school gate as she usually did. Instead, furious, she walked straight into town, down the High Street and into a large department store. She stomped up the stairs and into a fashion area selling clothes, shoes and jewellery. Liz wondered what she would steal today.

The class need to agree what Liz is going to steal and set up the area by organising where the till is, where the skirts hang, and so on. The scene should be constructed up to the moment of theft. They must decide where Liz enters and what she will do. A pupil should take the role of Liz and wander into the boutique as agreed. The rest of the class should comment and make suggestions, such as 'Why don't you pretend to look at some jeans first, but actually be watching the shop assistant?' Someone will need to take the part of the shop assistant. The class must decide whether or not Liz goes into the changing room. They may wish to place a few other customers in the area.

When all is agreed and everyone knows what is taking place, the teacher asks everyone to become customers. They'll need to be reminded to be aware of Liz's actions and to keep those as the focus for attention in their scene. The scene is played out.

The scene progresses and at the moment that Liz is stealing, the teacher, in role as a store detective, says loudly, *Stop!* (The 'Stop' will have the effect of stopping the class and getting their attention, as well as stopping Liz in the fictional context.)

 Extending ideas, group discussion and moving ideas forward

Two conscience alleys: Liz is caught

Stand behind Liz, put a hand upon her shoulder as though you are a security officer, and announce loudly:

You'd better come with me to the manager's office.

Conscience alley one
Explain to the class that you will walk Liz through the shop floor. As you do, each customer in turn should say aloud his or her reaction to what has taken place as Liz passes.
Examples are:

● *She ought to be thoroughly ashamed.*
● *I wonder what will happen to her now.*

Conscience alley two
Ask the class to form two lines about a metre and a half apart, facing each other. Explain that the store security guard takes Liz through a long corridor towards the manager's office. As she walks, thoughts are spinning around in her head. The pupil playing Liz will walk down the corridor of children turning to each one in turn from one side to the other. As Liz looks at each, he or she voices one of the thoughts that might be in Liz's mind (see Figure 10.3).

```
                              x        x
                              x        x
                              x        x
My mum's going to kill me                    Why didn't I listen to Emma?
                              x        x
                              x        x
                              x        x

                                  x
                                 Liz
```

Figure 10.3

Write a stream of consciousness extract for Liz, whose mind is full of fears for the future, past conversations and recent actions. An extract from a Virginia Woolf novel could illustrate how the text jumps from one thing to another to represent the mind

In pairs, read each other's extracts and give responses to what sense and atmosphere has been created

Interview: questioning Liz

Place one chair in the centre of the space and either the teacher or a volunteer is chosen to sit on it to represent Liz. All the others stand around the chair in a circle.

They question Liz, not as in real life, but in any order, perhaps overlapping, and never giving Liz time to reply. After the first few questions Liz tries to reply but gradually she is given less chance to do so. Teacher explains at the outset that the questions become louder and louder. The 'interrogators' could also move closer and closer to Liz. There needs to be an agreed signal to end the questioning. It might be that Liz shouts out 'I'm sorry!' The aim is to create what would be quite an alarming and disturbing scene, to demonstrate the seriousness of this type of behaviour.

Creating atmosphere by use of volume, pace and tone of voice

Could things have been different?

Teacher's intentions

- To invite consideration of responsibility for others;
- To reflect on the subject of the drama.

There is a range of ways that the class might reflect on the drama so far. It is helpful to let the children guide you on the areas they wish to pick up since these may reflect their own contexts. Suggestions of what is often suggested are below, with ways they can be approached.

Discussion and whole-class improvisation with corporate role

Ask the class what might have made things different.
They may suggest that:

- *Emma could have been firmer with Liz;*
- *The teacher should have spoken to Liz;*
- *Other classmates could have said more and not just accepted sweets.*

Ask them to consider the risks of firmer action:

- *Liz may have been given money by a visiting relation and was not stealing;*
- *Liz may have reacted badly to further probing by others.*

Children discuss the options and take roles to experiment on how things might have been. Rather than giving one child the full responsibility of the difficult role of Liz, you may wish to use corporate role, as in activity one (above). Thus children share the voice of Liz and build on each other's contributions.

 Considering different viewpoints and options

Discussion and improvisation: conversations giving reasons for actions

Why was Liz stealing?
Children consider reasons with one child or a corporate role for Liz and you and/or children questioning her.

Whole-group improvisation or freeze frame: Liz is taken home

Scenes of Liz being taken home by the police or speaking to a parent may be tried in groups or as a class.

Paired improvisation: conversations between Liz and Emma

Pupils may want to create the next conversation between Liz and Emma.

Journalistic writing

Look at items from local newspapers or newspaper websites on court cases which refer to theft.

Ask children to write an article that might have appeared in the newspaper about the problems of theft among young people.

Choose what sort of position to hold – are you a more traditional person who would bring back smacking or a young person who feels there is too much pressure on young people to have fashionable items?

In small groups question each other for opinions to help prepare material for the articles.

Prepare readings of pieces to others.

 Journalistic writing in an opinion piece

Reading aloud a non-fiction text

Reflection: what have we learned?

Discuss the consequences of Liz's actions. Try not to personalize the discussion at first, but raise questions about how things could have been different in this drama. The discussion could then widen to debate what the children could do in similar situations.

Chapter 11
Where's the Blame?

Working from the first scene of David Calcutt's *The Terrible Fate of Humpty Dumpty* (part of the *Dramascripts* series published by Nelson Thornes, Cheltenham, 1998, extract given below), in which a bullied schoolboy is accidentally electrocuted on a pylon, the children go back in time to look at what led to this tragedy. They are invited to explore both the minds of the 'gang' and the bullied Terry, and, most significantly, the responsibility of those who were silent observers.

Learning objectives

- To recognize language variation according to context and purpose;
- To understand the consequences of antisocial and aggressive behaviours.
- To consider the responsibility of being a member of a community.

Themes

- Bullying
- Social responsibility
- Empathy.

Resources

- David Calcutt's *The Terrible Fate of Humpty Dumpty,* scenes one and two (see fig 11.1 p. 95).

Time

- Three hours – three lessons each of one hour.

Notes

Don't let the horrific notion of an electrocuted child put you off this drama. Children deal with it very well and the shock of the dramatic event takes them quickly into a serious approach to the work. We recommend the play for a class reader. Ensure that the parts of Terry, Stubbs and Pete are not read by children who might be identified as bullied or bullies. Choose the latter for the character of Sammy, the protector of Terry Dumpton.

Creating scene one with the whole class

Teacher's intentions

- To set the scene;
- To encourage consideration of how the body communicates, as well as words;
- To highlight contrasts in personal experiences.

All elements of this activity should be taught in one session, and may take an hour.

Play reading: the first scene

Each child is given a copy of scene one and parts are allocated (fig 11.1 p. 95). The remaining children read for the gang. The stage directions are read with feeling by the teacher to create the haunting atmosphere.

> Reading play scripts

Discussion and practical exploration: exploring intimidation

In this activity, words are not relevant. Consideration is given to how the gang members may have made Terry feel intimidated without the use of words or physical contact. Teacher or a confident pupil stands in the centre of the space and invites volunteers one at a time to stand up and try out an intimidating role. They may stand and stare, they may circle, they may smile in a mocking manner. After each individual's attempt there is discussion about the effect and why it was or wasn't successful. They can explore the effect of physical distance between the two characters, the effect of height, what can be achieved with fast and slow movements and so on.

It is worth noting that the person creating the intimidation could honestly claim, 'I didn't touch him. I didn't say a word!'

Whole-group devising: the wasteground

Discuss what might have led up to the moment where the play begins.

- *Who had been at the wasteground first?*
- *At what point was Terry aware of the presence of the gang?*
- *How did they make their presence felt?*
- *Had Terry tried to get away, tried to join in, tried to look relaxed, or shown his fear?*

Agree some details and then create the scene of Terry and the gang meeting on the wasteground before any words are spoken. This depicts what took place immediately prior to the first scene of the play. No words are spoken in this scene and no physical contact is made. Pupils should draw on their intimidation experimentations. The challenge is to create a genuinely intimidating atmosphere, involving everyone, which makes what happens next in the script believable.

The pupils can circle, look threatening, circle and stare in order to lead to the moment where the dialogue begins.

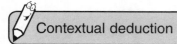
Contextual deduction

Whole-group performance of text: the pylon

The devised intimidation scene is then followed by the enactment of scene one from the script. First agree on what represents the pylon. It could be a chair or a table. Prepare by experimenting and modeling ways to enable Terry to climb the pylon slowly enough to build tension, looking up and down, asking the children how effective different gestures might be. The class agrees on how they will show the moment that he dies – for instance, he flops suddenly from the waist. Only then, hand over the role to a child.

In preparing to perform the scene, the 'gang' is encouraged to contribute vocally, such as 'yeahs', to continue the threatening atmosphere. Pauses between bits of dialogue need to be considered so that there is not just one line after another. Pete may look around the space before throwing the frisbee, so that there is a gap in speech at this point. This would draw attention to the moment when he throws it up into the pylon.

The two scenes can then be run together as one.

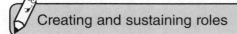
Creating and sustaining roles

Whole-group performance and thought tracking: Humpty's thoughts

About six volunteers are positioned on chairs around the edge of the space. The scenes will be run again, but this time the action is controlled by those on the chairs. When any one of them claps their hands, the action – whatever is taking place – freezes at once. The volunteer who has clapped speaks aloud a thought that Terry may have at that moment.

- *Why are they all here now?*
- *Maybe if I do this for them, they will leave me alone.*
- *My hands are slipping on the metal – I won't make it.*

After each thought, there is a moment's pause, and then the action continues again until the next clap is heard. The volunteers need to clap a few times for it to be most effective in slowing down the action and inviting scrutiny on what took place and the contrast between the individual's thoughts and the spoken words. It doesn't matter how close to each other the claps are.

Selecting vocabulary and syntax to communicate complex meanings

Children write diary entries of characters from the play

Read diaries aloud, contrasting those of different characters. Sammy's diary could be read one sentence at a time alternating with Stubbs's diary, read a sentence at a time, juxtaposing distinctions

The aftermath and implications of Terry's death

Teacher's intentions

● To consider the implications of actions;
● To understand how desperation can lead to desperate actions.

Class play reading: scene two

Read the second scene, with parts allocated (p. 95–7). Again, teacher reads the stage directions.

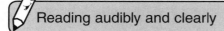

Reading audibly and clearly

Thought tapping: hearing Stubbs' thoughts

What might Stubbs be thinking on seeing Terry die?

A few suggestions are offered and discussed. The next activity is to explore the range and rush of thoughts, feelings and fears that will fill Stubbs's head.

Terry is positioned hanging on the 'pylon'. The gang is spread about the space at the moment Terry has just died. Stubbs is asked to move between the others, turning and twisting to represent his mind moving from one thought to another. He should stop in front of one gang member after another. As he does, the gang member responds by speaking aloud a thought that could be in Stubbs's mind:

● *Will Sammy grass on us?*
● *I've gone too far this time.*
● *Dumpton wasn't that bad.*
● *Why did he go on climbing?*
● *It was his fault.*

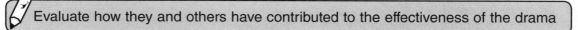

Evaluate how they and others have contributed to the effectiveness of the drama

Statementing: warning Sammy not to talk

Sammy has been identified as the weak link. He is seated in the centre of the space. The rest of the children stand around at some distance, as gang members. They have gathered together to ensure that Sammy will not say a word to anyone about what happened.

Each one moves forward in turn to Sammy and voices a threat. Stubbs should be the first to move in. Having said their lines, each moves back to keep Sammy looking isolated and giving room for the next member to go in.

● *You tell and you'll get it.*
● *Don't forget that you were there too.*
● *You say a word and we'll tell them how you forced Terry up there.*

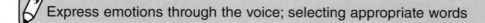

Express emotions through the voice; selecting appropriate words

The children write the story of *The Terrible Fate of Humpty Dumpty* from the point of view of a character in the story. For example, the children decide what Stubbs's version of events would be and write about them as if they were Stubbs

Previous bullying incidents and Sammy's statement

Teacher's intentions

- To create Terry's past experiences of bullying;
- To develop small-group work.

Small-group improvisation and performance: Terry's previous experiences

Tell the class that Sammy was left thinking back to what had gone before. He remembers so many incidents where Terry was teased, threatened and bullied by the gang.

- *What sort of incidents might these be?*

Small groups devise scenes that depict earlier incidents. They may take place in the playground after school, in the classroom or elsewhere. Each scene should freeze at the moment when the bullying behaviour peaks to maximum. These are performed.

Discussion should focus on how convincing the scenes were and whether they achieved feelings among the audience. Groups discuss any improvements they wish to make. These scenes will be used within the next activity.

 Group discussion with relevant contributions; listening and qualifying thoughts

Whole-class performance: Terry's experiences of bullying

Now the group scenes are brought together into one drama. Teacher in role is Sammy seven months later, when at last he has decided to make a statement. He is sitting on a chair, recalling the events from when Terry first joined the school, and he describes the incidents that led up to his death. Sammy recalls each of the incidents in the devised scenes, but instead of describing them, the groups get up and perform them.

The class arrange themselves in a horseshoe either side of him and are told before Sammy begins in which order the groups will perform. Teacher in role as Sammy provides the narrative which links the scenes and ends with reference to the wasteland. Below is a brief example of how it should be played.

It seems like yesterday that Terry moved into the area. We sat next to each other in Science and got on pretty well. He was shy, but fun ... I knew things were going to be hopeless for him on that first lunchtime. Stubbs came up and stood right in front of him in the lunch queue. 'What yer going to do about it?' Terry had no answer and let him go in front. Stubbs laughed and brought all his gang in front, too. I knew that was it. Terry's life would be hell.

The next day, he was in the playground ...

Then the scene in the playground is performed.

That's how it was. Then there was the time ...

And so on through the scenes.

And then the next time we all saw him was on the waste ground ...

Sammy covers his face with his hands, and can say no more.

 Participate in range of types of drama activity

The children write characters' school reports, e.g. 'Sammy seems to lack concentration in English at the moment. His work is untidy and full of careless mistakes. This is unusual for Sammy and causing me concern.' These can be collated in small groups, each taking different subjects

Who is to blame?

Teacher's intentions

- To consider Terry's behaviour;
- To consider what others think of bullies;
- To consider the responsibility of the bystanders.

Advice forum and teacher in role:

Teacher explains that Sammy wishes he had helped Terry. He could have given him some advice about how to survive Stubbs and his gang.

- *What advice would have been useful to Terry?*

The class is invited to offer Terry the advice that Sammy might have given. Teacher will enter as Terry, with shoulders down and eyes to the ground. Teacher needs to respond to the suggestions, which may include:

- *Hold your head up.*
- *Keep out of their way.*
- *Look Stubbs straight in the eye.*

Terry may attempt to act on what they say:

- *Do you mean stand like this?*
- *What sort of expression should I have when I look at him?*
- *Does this walk look okay?*

He may also reply that he can't, or doesn't know if the suggestion would work. The children may need to think very carefully about what will work. Teacher as Terry will need to react if inappropriate advice is offered.

Note that, for the teacher, it is fascinating that when this takes place in the classroom those who are bullied are often hearing from those who bully them what sort of things may put an end to bullying. It is a public discussion about what happens between the children, but it is neatly concealed as a drama about a pretend boy. It is therefore safe to discuss. We believe that it is best not to relate bullying incidents in the drama to 'real-life' incidents in your school. The children may if they wish, but otherwise they will take from it what they need to take for themselves.

 Finding appropriate language to deliver advice in very sensitive context

Statementing: thoughts about Stubbs

Class stands in a circle. Place a chair in the centre. It should remain empty, representing Stubbs.

No one would ever say what they thought of Stubbs. They wouldn't dare! Stubbs was too powerful. But what if, for one moment, they dared ... What would they say if they dared just once to tell Stubbs what they really thought of him?

Teacher demonstrates what they will all do: walk into the circle, up to the chair, and speak as though the chair is Stubbs before returning to their place in the circle. For instance:

- *You think we like you, but we don't.*
- *Do you ever think what it's like on the other side?*

Whole-group freeze frame and thought tap: the onlookers

Ask one of the small groups to recreate the frozen moment of bullying from the end of their scene. A playground scene is ideal. The remaining children stand in a circle around the edge of the space. They are asked to imagine that they were children in the playground that day and are reminded that everyone knew exactly what was going on.

- *Where were you standing at this moment when Terry was bullied?*
- *Did you watch?*
- *Did you pretend it wasn't happening?*
- *Did you point it out to your friend?*
- *Were you laughing at it?*
- *Were you running away so as not to get involved?*
- *Did you hope not to be seen by the bullies in case it was you next?*
- *Were you glad they were on to Terry so you were safe?*

One at a time and in silence, children move into the space and position themselves in an appropriate gesture, indicating a response to questions above. No one should move until the previous person has held his or her position and there has been time to consider his or her place in the overall context.

Teacher moves through the final creation and taps individuals on the shoulder. In response the child speaks aloud his or her imagined thoughts at this moment. Perhaps:

- *Terry is a weakling.*
- *They have no feelings.*
- *If it wasn't him, it would be me.*

Finally, teacher announces that all of them witnessed the bullying of Terry Dumpton. Not one of them did anything. What excuse do they have?

Spend time on a discussion of the responsibility of the onlookers in Terry's suffering. What could they have done?

 Exploring the ways that language varies with tone and pitch

Reflection: What have we learned?

Teacher's intentions

- To reflect on how things could be different;
- To challenge children into thinking of alternatives;
- To invite thoughts on responsible behaviour regarding bullying.

Freeze frames: changing the outcome

The small groups re-form and discuss how their image could be changed from the moment of peak tension. They can consider the advice given to Terry earlier or at any other moment in the drama, consider that other children didn't all actually support what Stubbs did to Terry and the fact that observers have responsibility. Their task is to change the dynamic in some way that means that Terry emerges 'unscathed' by moving from the frozen moment in a way that may be unexpected.

They show their new scenes and discuss the implications of the 'ways out' for Terry.

- *Would they work in real life?*
- *Would there be any repercussions later?*
- *What could they do differently when they see bullying behaviour in the future?*

To enable reflection of what has been learned without approaching reality, the following activity is recommended.

The children imagine that they work for a film promotions company and have been asked to create a film that can be used in schools to help combat bullying. They can make up anti-bullying rhymes, catchphrases and songs. They could choose to include discussion or interviews with those connected with the well-known Terry Dumpton case

The Terrible Fate of Humpty Dumpty by David Calcutt

SCENE 1

*(On the waste ground. **Stubbs,** with the **Members of his Gang** – **Jimmy, Pete, Kathy, Kay, Janet** and **Tracey** – are surrounding **Terry Dumpton. Sammy** stands to one side. **The Group** suddenly comes to life as the introductory music fades)*

Pete: (to Terry)	See my frisbee, Humpty? My best frisbee, this is. I've had this frisbee for ages. I love it. I'd hate to lose it. I'd go mad if I lost this frisbee. Want to see how it works? *(**Pete** throws the frisbee into the air, then he says)* Oh dear, it's got stuck in the pylon. What am I going to do now?
Stubbs:	You'll have to get it back, Pete.
Pete:	I know. Only trouble is, I'm scared of heights. Can't stand them. I get a nosebleed just going to the top of the stairs.
Stubbs:	You'll have to get somebody to fetch it down for you, then.
Pete:	That's right. Who though? *(**Stubbs** points to **Terry**)*
Stubbs:	Him! *(There is a pause. Then **Stubbs** says)* All right Humpty? Up you go. Get Pete's frisbee back for him. *(There is tension, then **Stubbs** continues)* Go on. Climb the pylon. Get it back. *(**Terry** stares up at the pylon. **Stubbs** goes on)* Perhaps you ain't our mate, then. Perhaps you don't like us at all. That means you're the kind of person who'd sneak on us. *(He walks towards **Terry**)*
Terry:	All right. I'll get it.
Sammy:	Don't, Terry.
Stubbs:	Shurrup, Sammy.
Sammy:	It's dangerous.
Kathy:	You wanna go up there instead? *(There is a pause)*
Stubbs:	Go on. *(**Terry** starts to climb the pylon. Egged on by **Pete**, the **Members of the Gang** start to chant 'Humpty Dumpty!' over and over again, and then shout comments up at **Terry**. **Sammy** runs forward)*
Sammy:	Don't, Terry. Come down.
Stubb:	Shurrup, Sammy, unless you wanna go up after him. *(The noise continues. Lights suddenly flash on and off. **Terry** hangs dead from the pylon. The **Members of the Gang** stare up in silence)*

SCENE 2

*(The **Members of the Gang** turn away from the pylon. They are excited and scared)*

Jimmy:	Stubbs, what we gonna do?
Janet:	Did you see him?
Tracey:	He was just hanging there.
Pete:	Perhaps he's just having us on. Just a joke, you know.
Kathy:	Don't be stupid. You saw the flash.

Tracey:	It was an accident. That's what it was, wasn't it? It was just an accident.
Kay:	Course, yeah. That's what it was, wasn't it? It was just an accident.
Pete:	He was just hanging there. Just hanging there. Like a fried egg! A fried egg! Get it?
	(**Pete** *laughs*)
Jimmy:	Shurrup, will you? Stop laughing. I said stop laughing!
	(*He pushes* **Pete**)
Pete:	Gerroff, Jimmy.
Jimmy:	Stop laughing, then, will you?
Pete:	All right, I've stopped.
Kathy:	Will you two stop it?
Pete:	It's him, throwing his weight around.
Kathy:	Just stop it. You're getting on my nerves.
Kay:	And mine.
Jimmy:	What we gonna do, Stubbs? Tell us. What we gonna do?
Janet:	I want to go home. I don't want to stay here. I'm going home.
Kathy:	No you ain't. You're staying here.
Janet:	You can't stop me.
Kathy:	Want a bet?
Kay:	Yeah, want to bet?
Stubbs:	Will you all just shurrup? I'm trying to think.
Kay:	It's about time.
Stubbs:	And you Kathy. Knock it off. We gotta think what to do.
Tracey:	It was an accident wasn't it? It wasn't our fault.
Stubbs:	That's right. It was an accident. It wasn't nothing to do with us. We wasn't even here.
Jimmy:	What do you mean Stubbs? We wasn't here?
Pete:	Listen to what he's got to say, thickhead.
Jimmy:	Don't call me thickhead.
Kathy:	For God's sake, will you two shurrup?
Stubbs:	Right. Listen. This is the story. We wasn't here. We was somewhere else. Down the town. Right? We don't know what happened. We don't know anything about it. Anybody asks us, that's what we tell them. We wasn't here.
Kathy:	That's your idea, is it?
Stubbs:	Yeah. Why? You got a better one?
Pete:	What about my frisbee?
Stubbs:	Your what?
Pete:	My frisbee.
Tracey:	Dumpton's dead, and all he can think about is his frisbee.
Pete:	It's important. My frisbee's still up there.
Stubbs:	Has it got your name on it?
Pete:	No …
Stubbs:	Well, it don't matter then, does it?
Jimmy:	Thickhead.
Janet:	We ought to phone for an ambulance. We ought to tell somebody.
Pete:	Ambulance ain't no good for him now. It's a hearse he needs.
Janet:	You're sick, you are.
Tracey:	Janet's right. We ought to tell somebody. The police.

Stubbs:	We ain't telling nobody!
Janet:	We can't just leave him up there.
Stubbs:	You wanna drop us all in it? Is that what you want? You know what'll happen if they find out.
Kathy:	Stubbs is right. We've all gotta stick together now. Stick to the same story. That's the only thing we can do.
Kay:	Yeah. That's right.
Stubbs:	Everybody agreed then? Right?
Janet:	I suppose so. As long as I can go home. I don't feel very well.
Kathy:	You can go home now. Just make sure you don't say anything.
Janet:	I won't.
Tracey:	I'm coming with you.
	(*Janet* and *Tracey* go)
Pete:	I'm going as well. See you tomorrow.
Stubbs:	See you, Pete.
	(*Pete* goes)
Kathy:	(*Pointing to* **Sammy**). What about him?
Stubbs:	Leave him to me. He won't be no trouble.
Kathy:	Just make sure of it.
Stubbs:	I will!
Kathy:	Come on Kay.
	(*Kathy* and *Kay* go)
Stubbs:	You got the story straight, Sammy?
Sammy:	What?
Stubbs:	Got the story? We weren't here.
Sammy:	We killed him.
Stubbs:	I'm warning you.
Sammy:	We killed him. It was us. We did that.
Stubbs:	Jimmy. See to him.
	(*Jimmy* grabs **Sammy**. Then **Stubbs** says)
	Now listen, Sammy. You're in this with the rest of us. So don't you go talking to anybody about it. Right? 'Cos if you do, it ain't just the police you'll have to worry about. You'll have to worry about Jimmy here making such a mess of your face that nobody'll ever recognise you again. They won't even know if you was a human being. Ain't that right Jimmy?
Jimmy:	Yeah. That's right.
Stubbs:	So just remember, Sammy. Remember whose side you're on.
	(*There is a pause. Then* **Stubbs** says)
	Come on Jimmy.
	(*Jimmy* looses **Sammy**)
Jimmy:	Remember, Sammy.
	(*Stubbs* and *Jimmy* go. Then **Sammy** looks up at **Terry's** body)
Sammy:	Terry … I'm sorry … I tried to help but … I'm sorry
	(*He faces the* **Audience**, *and says*)
	We killed him!
	(*He runs off*)

Figure 11.1 *The Terrible Fate of Humpty Dumpty* by David Calcutt. Extract reproduced by kind permission of Nelson Thornes Ltd. © Nelson Thornes Ltd.

Chapter 12
The Mysteries of the World

A strange advertisement appears in the paper. Whoever wrote it must be crazy! We are all invited to attend a meeting to discover the secrets of the world. Given crystal balls, we all see images of other times emerge through swirling mists. The children write poems about what they saw and they are presented on top of illustrations of the vision. A fun, whimsical drama!

Learning objectives

- To practise formal letter writing;
- To practise formal speaking;
- To explore language in poetry writing;
- To practise persuasive language.

Themes

- Mystery
- Fantasy.

Resources

- White board/flip chart/PowerPoint with the advertisements displayed;
- A sheet of paper per child with a large pre-drawn circle to represent a crystal ball (the poems will be written inside this parameter);
- Crayons.

Time

- Three hours in total, but this depends upon the time given to presenting/performing the poetry.

A strange advertisement in the newspaper

Teacher's intentions

- Interpreting a newspaper advertisement;
- Writing a formal letter.

Reading and discussion

Display the following, explaining that it is a made-up advertisement. It is imagined that this was found in a newspaper.

> *If any of you noble readers wish to know all the mysteries of the beginning of the world, write to me, Lydia Rose Dawlish, Park Mansion, Slapton-Heydon, Somerset. Please explain why you wish to know the great mysteries and if there is anything in which you are particularly interested.*

Teacher-led discussion:

- *What could this mean?*
- *What might Lydia be like?*
- *What clues are there in the advertisement?*
- *Who might reply to such a notice?*
- *What would Lydia expect to see in a letter responding to the advertisement?*

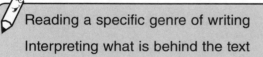

> Reading a specific genre of writing
>
> Interpreting what is behind the text

> Look at newspapers to see examples of advertisements

Formal letter writing

Pupils are invited to reply to the advertisement. You may need to demonstrate the appropriate layout for letter writing. Children will have fun responding to this strange advertisement. Some pupils may wish to read their replies, and/or they may be displayed.

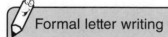

> Formal letter writing
>
> Responding to an advertisement in written form

> Look at letter writing formats on computer programmes
>
> Look at examples of formal and informal letters
>
> Look at the way letters were written in previous times

Paired improvisation and overheard conversations: should we go or not?

Display and discuss what appeared in the newspaper the following week.

> *To all those who answered my advertisement. Please attend a meeting at The Seven Seas Hotel, Bristol on Thursday, 5 March.*

Children work in pairs. As are keen to attend the meeting and try to persuade Bs, who are reluctant. Bs may choose to be cynical, frightened, too busy. Snippets of the conversations are shared with the class.

Using persuasive language

Look up where Bristol is on a map (hard or electronic) and describe directions from London, for example. Could be oral or written instructions

Meeting with Lydia Rose Dawlish

Teacher's intentions

- To improvise an extraordinary and magical meeting;
- To create subject matter for poetry writing.

Whole-class improvisation with teacher in role

Explain to the class that they all eventually agreed to go. Those who were not sure have since been persuaded. This is to ensure everyone can be involved in the drama.

The classroom needs to be arranged so that the pupils sit in a horseshoe, preferably behind desks or tables. The teacher takes the role of the slightly eccentric Lydia Rose Dawlish, welcoming her visitors with authority, and along the following lines:

I welcome you all. I respect you all for your earnest curiosity, and I am delighted to say that all you noble people will be rewarded for your trouble getting here. I tell you all that any who take this endeavour with sincerity will see visions from the past on this very day. Every one of you has been carefully selected. You have all proved to me that you have a genuine desire to know the mysteries of the world. Perhaps it would be a good idea if some of you introduced yourselves to the others and explained your particular interests.

I should, of course, start with myself, Lydia Rose Dawlish [said with great pride]. I have been bestowed with a wondrous gift. I, Lydia Rose Dawlish, can see into the past, and I have even had some hazy glimpses into the future. Not only have I the special powers to do all this, but I also have the powers to enable all who truly yearn to see the past for themselves. You will not regret coming here today.

Now, let's start with you. Tell us about yourself. Please stand to address this very special gathering.

Some children are invited to introduce themselves, perhaps making up eccentric-sounding names, sharing their reasons for coming and their expectations of the meeting.

Listening and finding appropriate oral response for the specific context

Look at character descriptions used in play texts, e.g. write what might appear for Lydia

Prepare descriptions of the sort of character who speaks as Lydia does

Storytelling: looking into the crystal ball

Lydia then explains that she will hand out the (imaginary) crystal balls. As they are given out, each person is instructed to place his or her hands either side of the crystal ball, palms down. Lydia hands them out one at a time, in an earnest manner!

Back in her seat in front of everyone, Lydia tells of the way things must be done. They people are to keep their eyes on their own crystal ball and keep their hands in position. They must all repeat the words that she will say to lead them all to the mystery. Failure to achieve these things may affect their potential to see images of other times.

All repeat the words ... [e.g.] Hoola speeka rabinger ray ...

Lydia utters a little nonsense with great dignity! Keep this up until the words are spoken in earnest by the children.

Lydia then describes what she can see in her crystal ball:

... swirling mist of orange and purple ... it's weaving around itself ... Oh, now it's clearing a little ... there's still lots of orange ... but there is black, too ... the black is like a thick curtain ... Oh ... it is smoke! ... People are rushing about, screaming and shouting ... in a frenzy ... many are making for a huge river, they're getting water to try to put out the fire. I don't think it will help much as there is so much fire ... the buildings ...

Finally,

My image is fading, the black is fading, mist now, cloud ... the image in the crystal ball.
[This could be a more detailed description of the fire of London.]

The pupils then have the opportunity to describe what they see in their crystal balls. Some may use events they know of, others may be completely fictitious.

The meeting is closed in an appropriately ritualistic manner befitting the great Lydia Rose Dawlish. She collects the crystal balls, thanking the participants for their exciting revelations. Finally, she raises her hands into the air, announcing that all her readers are noble indeed and that she is delighted to have shared the mysteries with them.

Using imagination to create visions

Understanding how tone and choice of words shape meaning

Research descriptions of the fire of London

Poetry writing

Teacher's intentions

- To use the creative ideas from the drama for poetry writing;
- To consider atmosphere in words;
- To create presentation of poem within colourful crystal ball.

Creating crystal balls: the poetry writers

The children prepare to write poems to describe the visions they saw in their crystal balls. They will create a classroom display of crystal balls with colourful mists and illustrations as background to their poems.

Ask for words and phrases used in the drama to describe the scenes in the crystal balls, e.g. swirling mists,

Explain alliteration and ask for suggestions of other words that could be added to examples, e.g. swirling, sweeping mists, or swirling, meandering mists.

Talk about rhyme and non-rhyme in poetry.

Poetry writing

Step 1
Each child makes a list of phrases associated with their vision, using alliteration and perhaps lists appropriate rhymes.

Step 2
Hand out the sheets of paper with pre-drawn large circle drawn. Children use crayons to draw coloured mists or images appropriate to the story of their vision.

Step 3
Children write drafts of poems describing their visions and read them to each other, inviting comments and suggestions.

Step 4
Pupils each write their final draft poems in their prepared coloured circles/crystal balls.

Alliteration

Forms of poetry

Rhythm in words

Look up examples of poems that rhyme and those that do not. Consider what makes poems sound like poems when they do not rhyme

Presenting the poetry: reading aloud

There are options:
- Mount the crystal balls with poems and display in the school;
- Scan the crystal balls and create a display using ICT. Pupils could record their poems;
- Prepare display and live poetry reading for others.

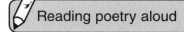

Reading poetry aloud

Listen to poetry read aloud, live or recorded

The journalist is a cynic

Teacher's intentions

● Encourage children to take a stand on their views – persuasive language;
● Consider headlines for the newspaper.

Teacher in role: the journalist

Explain that a journalist has gathered all those who attended some crazy woman's meeting at The Seven Seas Hotel in Bristol. Unless the noble readers can persuade the journalist that it was not nonsense, a nasty article will appear in tomorrow's paper, mocking Lydia Rose Dawlish and all who took part in it.

He or she doesn't believe that anyone really saw anything. Children, as noble readers who saw visions, try to convince teacher in role that it was all real.

 Using persuasive language

Maintaining a position in discussion

Consider how people hold arguments by looking at interviews on television or radio

Creating headlines: tomorrow's edition

What might have appeared in the newspapers the following day? Children discuss and write their headlines in large letters.

● *Mystical Power in Bristol*
● *Dafty Dawlish*
● *Fruitcake in Major Con* (a favourite from an eleven-year-old boy)

Children hold their suggestion up and announce them in appropriate voices.

 Considering newspaper headlines

Children cut out headlines and decide what attitude they wish to create in the reader. Read them with a voice to express this

Reflection: what have we learned?

Discuss the character of Lydia Rose Dawlish. How would they describe her? What have you learned about using your own imagination to develop ideas? What have we learned about poetry writing and formal letter writing?

Recommended Reading

Baldwin, P. (2004) *With Drama in Mind: Real Learning in Imagined Worlds*. Stafford: Network Educational Press.

Baldwin, P. (2008) *The Practical Primary Drama Handbook*. London: Paul Chapman.

Baldwin, P. and Fleming, K. (2002) *Teaching Literacy through Drama: Creative Approaches*. London: Routledge Falmer.

Booth, D. (1994) *Story Drama*. Markham, Ontario: Pembroke Publishing.

Bowell, P. and Heap, B. (2001) *Planning Process Drama*. London: David Fulton Publishers.

Clipson-Boyles, S. (2011) *Teaching Primary English through Drama: A practical and creative Approach*. David Fulton Books.

Dickinson, R. and Neelands, J. (2006) *Improve your Primary School through Drama*. London: David Fulton.

Farmer, D. (2011) *Learning Through Drama in the Primary Years*. Drama Resource.

Goodwin, J. (2006) Using Drama to Support Literacy: Activities for Children aged 7 to 14. London: Paul Chapman.

Haddon, J. (2009) *Teaching Reading Shakespeare*. London: Routledge

Miller, C. and Saxton, J. (2004) *Into the Story: Language in Action Through Drama*. Heinemann; Portsmouth, NH.

Prendiville, F. (2007) *Speaking and Listening Through Drama, 7–11*. London: Paul Chapman.

Saxton,J. and Miller, C.S. (2004) *Into the Story: Language in Action Through Drama*. Portsmouth, New Hampshire: Heinemann.

Tandy, M. (2010) *Creating Drama with 4–7 Year Olds: Lesson Ideas to Integrate Drama into the Primary Curriculum*. London: Routledge

Tandy, M. and Howell, J. (2009) *Creating Drama with 7–11 Year Olds: Lesson Ideas to Integrate Drama into the Primary Curriculum*. London: Routledge.

Winston, J. (2004) *Drama and English at the Heart of the Curriculum: Primary and Middle Year*. London: David Fulton

Winston, J. and Tandy, M. (2008) *Beginning Drama 4–11 (Early Years & Primary)*. London: David Fulton.

Winston, J. and Tandy, M. (2012) *Beginning Shakespeare 4–11*. London: Routledge.

Woolland, B. (2010) *Teaching Primary Drama*. Harlow: Pearson Longman.